SCALE MODEL
DETAILING

KALMBACH BOOKS

Publisher's Cataloging in Publication
(Prepared by Quality Books Inc.)

Scale model detailing / [edited by Terry Spohn].
      p. cm.
      Includes bibliographical references and index.
      ISBN 0-89024-209-7

      1. Models and modelmaking. I. Spohn, Terry, ed.

TT154.S33 1995   745.5'928
                            QBI95-20095

Printed in the United States of America.

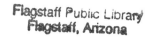

CONTENTS

DETAILING YOUR FIRST PLASTIC SHIP MODEL

Fig. 1. The Modelcraft *Pola* provided a good basis for adding detailing. The color scheme is especially eye-catching.

BY DENNIS MOORE

Detailing ship models is basically an exercise in adding new parts and replacing overscale items with finer pieces. By studying photographs, you can find many small details that can be added to your model. You can add as much detail as you want; in fact, most ship kits leave quite a lot of room for improvement.

For an example of basic ship detailing I've selected the R. M. *Pola,* a World War Two Italian cruiser in 1/400 scale. This size model (18 inches long) is large enough to make detailing easy. The kit was made by Modelcraft and is now a rare and expensive collector's item, but it's a good kit on which to illustrate basic detailing techniques.

Hull. The kit's hull was molded in two parts which join at the waterline, leaving the modeler with the option of a full hull or waterline model. I chose to build the waterline version. The main deck pieces fit into the hull and I used putty at

Fig. 2. Dennis used a piece of cardboard as a guide when painting the red stripes.

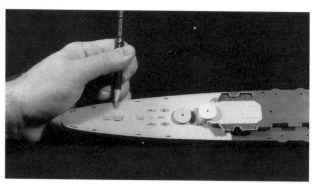

Fig. 3. To accentuate the wood deck detail a pencil was lightly grazed across the raised molding.

the bow and stern to fill slight gaps. Inserts on the side of the hull also required putty and sanding. It's important to get a good finish on the hull and a smooth sheer line.

Small parts such as davits, gangplanks, etc., are easily broken in handling, so it's better to clean them up and paint them while they're still on the sprue tree. I don't add these delicate parts until the model is nearly complete.

Painting. I paint a ship in stages. I assemble and paint major assemblies such as the bridge and shelter deck before attaching them to the hull. I used Pactra's International colors throughout: light gray for the hull and upper works, deck tan for the natural wood areas, dark gray for the metal areas of the deck, and insignia white and red for the barber pole section of the bow.

Painting the barber pole pattern on the bow is a problem because of the clutter molded on the deck. Masking tape didn't work, so I used stiff cardboard as a straightedge mask, Fig. 2. Even with the card, some touchup with a brush was required.

Decks. To highlight the spaces between wood deck planks, I used a soft lead art pencil (Eberhard Faber 4B). After painting the planking tan and allowing it to dry, I held the pencil at an angle and grazed the raised detail, Fig. 3. This darkens the raised outline of the planks; it's not important to hit all the raised areas because you're trying to create an overall visual effect. If you get stray pencil marks, simply touch up the deck color with a fine brush. Although the pencil marks look metallic, they will be fine once they are oversprayed with flat.

I glued the shelter deck assembly to the main deck, filling and

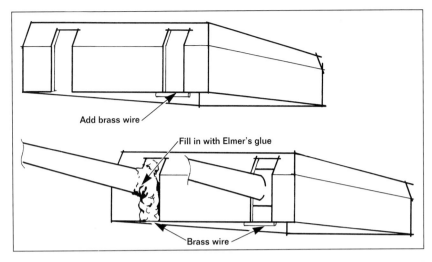

Fig. 4. Blast bags

Fig. 5. This close-up shows the gun shields and replaced funnel grilles. Note the effectiveness of the wood deck detailing.

sanding the area where it meets the fore deck. I used a small amount of Elmer's GlueAll to fill a crack at the joint under the "X" turret.

Guns. There is usually room for improving turrets and guns on warships; Pola was no exception. The main barbettes had peepholes in the faceplates which can be drilled out. I also drilled out the barrels of the main guns. I added blast bags on the main batteries by gluing fine brass wire under the bottom of the openings for the gun barrels, then painting Elmer's

into the openings and around the base of the barrels, Fig. 4. The wire helps keep the glue in place as it dries, so it will lie flat under the barrels.

There is a large opening in the splinter shields of the secondary batteries because they are dual-purpose (antiship and antiaircraft) guns. A light plate was usually installed over this opening, which would fold on top of the shield when the guns were fired. I made these plates out of thin sheet plastic, Fig. 5.

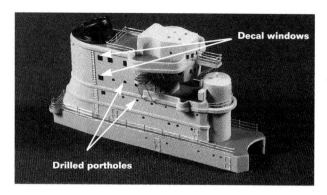

Fig. 6. A plain bridge structure was highlighted with added windows, portholes, ladders, and railing.

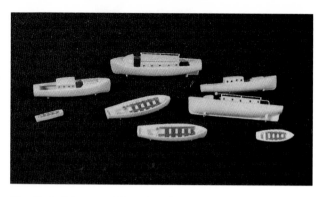

Fig. 7. Railings and interior details improved the ship's boats. A few added details and painting can bring small parts to life.

Funnels. The funnel caps had new grilles made with HO wire from Detail Associates. I bent the spine of the grille over a paintbrush handle and cut it to size. After gluing the spine into place with Elmer's, I added the rest of the grille wires, Fig. 5. I used a drafting compass to measure the lengths of the wires, and find it a helpful tool in ship construction.

Bridge details. I added windows to the bridge using black decal striping. The peep openings on the range-finders were drawn on with the art pencil after painting, Fig. 6. I also used the pencil to highlight ladders, hatches, and similar structures throughout the ship. I drilled out searchlights on both the bridge and funnel scaffold and filled them with Micro Kristal-Kleer. Photo-

etched brass railings and ladders were added where appropriate. I had to enlarge several holes to allow braces for the bridge top to fit. Test fitting parts will allow you to find these problems.

More details. I detailed the ship's boats by adding HO brass wire for oars, drilling out portholes, and adding railings to the two barges, Fig. 7. These railings were scraps left over from those used on the bridge. I also used scrap rails on the range-finder platform and the crow's nest. Brass wire was used to provide stronger flagstaffs on the bow and stern.

When all the assemblies above deck had been completed, I glued them in place, except for the tripod mast assembly and guns. It was easier to install the railings on the

main deck without these parts in place. I used photoetched brass parts for all the railings on the R. M. *Pola*.

Anchor chains. Adding or replacing molded-in chain with the real thing is an easy way to improve the look of most ship models. Campbell Scale Models Detailing Chain (No. 256) provided anchor chain, which I used in addition to that provided in the kit, Fig. 8. I cut the chains, painted them black, and attached them using Elmer's painted lightly on the deck.

Rigging. I oversprayed the entire ship with Micro Flat. Clear stretched sprue was handy for rigging because clear sprue's appearance is more delicate than colored sprue. I measured the distances between points using the drafting

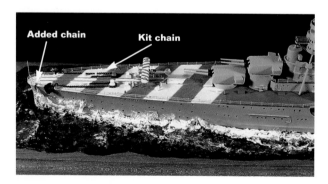

Fig. 8. Dennis added the strand of chain forward of the anchor. Real chain always improves a ship model. The kit aircraft benefited from careful painting and detailing.

Fig. 9. Even the raised gangplanks had detailed awnings added. The flag was made from a decal. Note the searchlights with Kristal-Kleer lenses.

compass again. After cutting the sprue, I glued it into place using Elmer's glue and a paintbrush.

The Italian flag wasn't provided in the kit, but I made it from a Microscale 1/72 scale decal sheet for Italian aircraft. I cut a rudder tricolor to the right size, folded it over, and then placed the House of Savoy's crest in the middle of the white bar.

Gangplanks. Working from photos, I added step-on-and-off plates at the top and bottom of the kit gangplanks and drilled holes for guardrails and canopy supports. Gangplank railings weren't provided in the photoetched set, so I bent the straight handrails slightly to give a slant to the stanchions. Some brands of railings include railings for gangplanks and stairs.

Next, I made guardrails and the canopy assembly from brass wire. I made the tiny awnings from paper cut to size, glued into place, then painted white, Fig. 9.

Photoetched brass railings. I decided to use photoetched brass railings for the first time on this model. I used railings and ladders made by Fred Hultberg's Fotocut. Using photoetched parts is not as complicated as it might appear.

The first step is to remove the brass from the film backing. This brand comes stuck to the backing sheet; newer brands don't have a film backing. Place the pieces in a dish, then cover them with lacquer thinner. You don't need to drown them; I use an eyedropper to apply just enough thinner to get them wet. Once you apply the thinner you'll notice the film begin to curl, almost like a decal dipped in water. The film eventually will straighten and the brass will come loose (Figs. 10 and 11). Don't remove too many lengths of railing

Fig. 10   **Fig. 11**

Fig. 12

at once; these pieces are delicate and can be lost or bent.

These railings had four rails; the bottom railing is designed to be glued directly to the deck, leaving three rails. I wanted mine shorter, so I removed one line of railing by cutting the stanchions with fine nail scissors.

When you have a bend in the deck, the railing will have to be bent to fit before it is applied. This can become difficult if the bend is combined with a curve. I found that bending a sharp angle works best using tweezers to hold the rail and provide the bending surface. A curve can be bent around a dowel or paintbrush handle. Be careful not to bend too far initially, as the railing may break if bent back.

Attach the railings with Elmer's glue brushed on the deck with a fine brush. Put them on after the major assemblies but

before adding final details (Fig. 12). Paint the railings after they are attached; this helps blend them in and hides glue marks.

At this point the finished model was ready to be mounted on its base. The water was made of acrylic gel, which was then painted and glazed using acrylic paints. These artist's gels are available in art supply stores and many hobby shops. The finished model shows how including easy-to-add details can improve the finished look of any ship model.

SOURCES

• **Chain:** Campbell Scale Models, c/o Wm. K. Walthers, Inc., P. O. Box 18676, Milwaukee, WI 53218
• **Photoetched railings:** Fotocut, c/o Fred Hultberg, Box 120, Erieville, NY 13061

PHOTOETCHED DETAILS FOR SMALL-SCALE SHIPS

How to handle and install those tiny metal bits

BY RUSTY WHITE

Detail is the name of the game in prizewinning ship models. Until recently, modelers could properly detail small scale vessels only with painstakingly scratchbuilt railings, inclined ladders, radar screens, catapults, and cranes. Facing this task, many would-be ship modelers were scared off.

Commercially available photoetched brass or stainless steel detail sets have changed all that. You no longer need a scratch-builder's skills to build realistic models. Most winning entries at IPMS regional and national competitions now feature photoetched details. Nearly all photoetched detail sets are cottage industry products. You can obtain them by mail order or at well-stocked hobby shops. Your first try. Using photoetched parts is easy compared to scratchbuilding all the detail. They do require a few tools, Fig. 4, and a lot of patience and manual dexterity. If your close-up vision isn't good, you'll need reading glasses or a good magnifying device.

Fig. 1. Imagine how barren this MRC-Tamiya 1/350 scale USS *Enterprise* would look without Gold Medal Models' photoetched brass railings and antennas.

Fig. 2. Cruisers like this Skywave USS *Vincennes* are ideal for your first attempt with photoetched details because they have straight sections of railing.

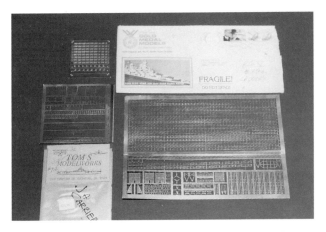

Fig. 3. Many ship details come from cottage industry manufacturers.

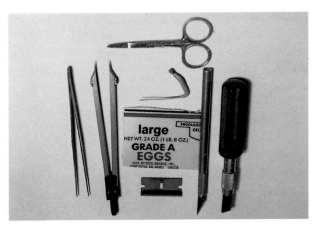

Fig. 4. You'll need a couple of knives, tweezers, draftsman's dividers, cuticle scissors, and a square cut from an egg carton.

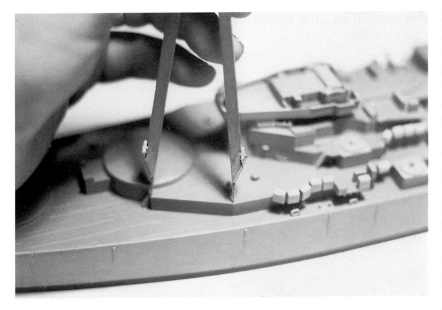

Fig. 5. Measure the length of railing section with draftsman's dividers.

Removing parts from the sheet. It's important to remove the parts only as you need them. They're small and easily lost. Place the carrier sheet on a piece of clear acrylic (Plexiglas), and cut the parts out with a new No. 11 blade. Score three or four times close to the part to avoid burrs. A bit more pressure with the knife should separate the part from the frame. File rough spots with a fine jeweler's file or 320-grit sandpaper. Go slowly and make sure you aren't inadvertently bending the parts as you hold them.

Measuring. Many photoetched detail sets include long railing sections that must be cut to length. How do you get your ruler into a tight corner when measuring these railings? I use draftsman's dividers to measure short distances. (Look for a set in an art supply store.) The long needle arms can fit almost anywhere on a ship model. Adjust the distance between the arms and measure the area to be railed, Fig. 5; to transfer the measurement, place the dividers on the railings and mark the ends, Fig. 6.

Bending. It's hard for beginners to make clean bends without distorting or cutting through the fragile

My techniques should save you a lot of trouble. Start with a 1/700 scale set on a cruiser such as Skywave's USS *Vincennes*. Cruisers feature many straight lines and few intricacies, Fig. 2. And a 1/700 scale detail set will set you back only $10 to $15. Working with the larger parts in a 1/350 scale set will be a breeze once you get used to handling photoetched parts in 1/700 scale.

Preparation. Your model should be about 95 percent complete and fully painted before you start working with detail parts. Leave delicate parts such as radars, antennas, and cranes for last. Study the detail set to see which details in the plastic kit can be replaced by photoetched parts.

Paint the entire sheet of photoetched parts in the main color of the model before removing any parts. Have extra paint on hand for touch-up: Every time you bend, cut, or file the parts, paint will chip, exposing shiny metal beneath.

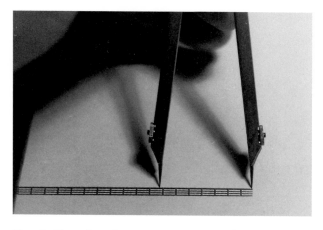

Fig. 6. Transfer the measurement to the railing and mark the ends.

Fig. 7. Pressing down with the chisel blade bends the railing as the soft plastic foam yields to the pressure.

photoetched parts. Most sets' instructions are vague on assembly technique.

This method works every time: First, make a work surface by cutting out a small square of thin plastic foam from an egg carton. Carefully place a No. 17 or 18 chisel blade where you want the fold. Now press gently until the part folds, Fig. 7. You can bend it to any angle with the right amount of pressure. If you go too far, carefully unfold the part with your fingers. This method works well with

Fig. 8. Bending the railing for circular decks can be tricky.

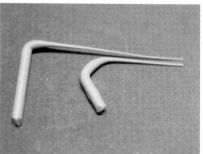

Fig. 10. SUPER GLUE PUDDLE

Super glue puddle

Upside-down paint bottle

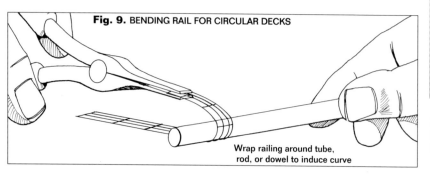

Fig. 9. BENDING RAIL FOR CIRCULAR DECKS

Wrap railing around tube, rod, or dowel to induce curve

Fig. 11. Rusty uses the styrene nubs left over from stretched sprue to apply tiny drops of super glue.

Fig. 12. Add fragile antennas, radars, and cranes last.

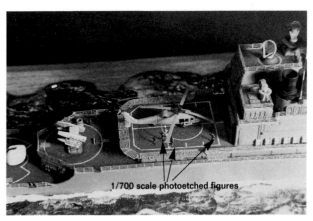

1/700 scale photoetched figures

Fig. 13. Populating your ships with tiny photoetched figures brings the model to life.

long narrow cranes, inclined ladders, and radio towers.

The more bends you make, the greater your chances of bending these thin metal parts in the wrong place. Except for straight stretches of rail, work with pieces only a few inches long.

Circular decks are the most challenging to rail. Worse, they seem to attract the most attention, Fig. 8. Since rail comes on the sheet flat, you must induce the curve into the parts. Wrap the rail around a cylindrical object such as a brass tube or wood dowel—even a round hobby knife handle works, Fig. 9. Use a cylinder or rod a little smaller than the curve you need: The metal's "memory" will make it uncurl slightly.

Application. Now comes the critical operation: attaching the detail parts. Ordinary plastic glues won't bond the metal. White glue (such as Elmer's Glue-All) works, but five-minute epoxy or super glue is best. I like gapfilling, fast-setting super glue. It's easier to control a single drop of the thicker gapfilling formula glues than the standard runny super glue. Fast setting helps too, since it's hard to maintain a steady hand while waiting for it to set.

I've developed a couple of makeshift tools for applying super glue. Instead of applying it direct from the container, I place a few drops in the concave bottom of an upside-down paint bottle, Fig. 10. Then I apply the glue with nubs left from stretching sprue, Fig. 11. The finer the point on the nub, the smaller the droplet of glue I can transfer. When dried super glue builds up on the tip, I shave it off with a sharp blade or make a new nub.

Apply all the railing first. Touch up the paint after you complete each area. You may not be able to reach some spots if you wait until the model is completed, so get them as you go along. Starting with the upper decks and working down will keep you

away from work already completed.

Proceed to the inclined ladders, vertical ladders, and yardarm rails. Assemble and apply cranes, catapults, radar, and antennas last, Fig. 12.

Extras. I laughed at the first 1/700 scale figures I saw: little guys less than 1/8" high who looked like Gumby. But after experimenting, I think they enhance the scale effect and bring models to life, Fig. 13.

You also shouldn't ignore the tiny 1/700 scale aircraft props, landing gear, and tail hooks on photoetched aircraft carrier detail sets. They're far superior to plastic airplane detail in this scale. Photoetched detail sets, along with practice and patience, will help you turn out ship models that rival museum quality.

SOURCES

• Flagship Models, 2204 Summer Way Lane, Edmond, OK 73013
• Gold Medal Models, 12332 Chapman Avenue, No. 81, Garden Grove, CA 92640
• Model Technologies, 13472 Fifth St., Suite 12, Chino, CA 91710

• Tom's Modelworks, 1050 Cranberry Drive, Cupertino, CA 95014
• Verlinden Products, VLS Mail Order, Lone Star Industrial Park, 811 Lone Star Dr., O'Fallon, MO 63366

BUILDING USS *MASSACHUSETTS* IN 1/225 SCALE

Improving and converting Glencoe's *Oregon*

Fig. 1. From the port bow, you can see the red-throated ventilators and the stretched-sprue rigging. Note the high rails of the main deck.

Fig. 2, right. The *Massachusetts* in 1910, soon after her refit. Naval History photo No. NH 63138.

BY BOB SANTOS

Years ago I scratchbuilt a large radio-controlled model of the USS *Massachusetts* as she appeared in 1900. I collected much information on her, including several sets of drawings, many photos, and several books. Converting the Glencoe (ITC) USS *Oregon* (BB3) to a *Massachusetts* (BB2), circa 1910, seemed simple. But though the kit includes the decal for *Massachusetts* and uses a soft, easy-to-cut plastic, I still had a great deal of work ahead.

Oregon, the only sister ship (*Indiana,* BB1, was the third) built on the West Coast, differed from the others in many ways. For an accurate *Massachusetts,* you must correct errors in the kit, reflect the differences between *Oregon* and *Massachusetts,* update the *Massachusetts* to her appearance in 1910, and generally enhance the detail all around.

Airbrush each subassembly before bringing them all together. The color scheme is simple: Wood decks are tan and all else above the waterline is gray. Below the waterline the ship is dark red with no boot topping. I used the kit's *Massachusetts* decals on both sides of the stern.

Fig. 3. Bob's *Massachusetts* started off as a Glencoe *Oregon*, but the superstructure underwent many modifications, including replacing much of the molded-on detail. Finished model photos by the author. In-progress photos by FSM photographer A. L. Schmidt.

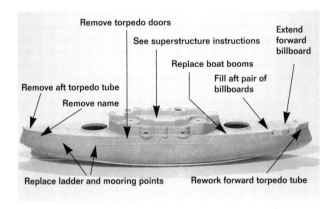

Fig. 4

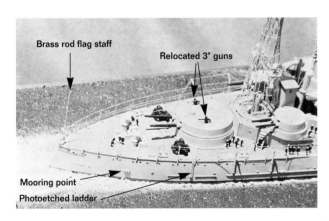

Fig. 6

Photos of *Massachusetts* in 1910 show no scrollwork or shield on the bow, and no draft numbers at the waterline. The gun and smokestack caps are all black, the starboard running light green, and the port running light red. I painted the ship's boats gray too, but I painted the covers a lighter shade to break up the monotony. The insides of all ventilators were red.

Hull details. To create a waterline model, remove the bottom of each hull half by cutting 1/16" below the waterline with a razor saw. Slice off the ship's name on the stern and the boat booms on the sides of the hull. *Massachusetts* had no after pair of anchor bays (billboards); remove the kit's and fill the holes after the hull halves are joined. I added billboard extensions from scrap plastic, opened all the cast-on ports, and drilled new ones where needed. Then I replaced much of the cast-on hull details and removed some of the details *Massachusetts* didn't have (Fig. 4).

Since *Massachusetts* had three anchors, remove the crane pad for the port aft crane and scratchbuild three anchor cranes. I rearranged and created new deck equipment—bitts, eyes, capstans, and so forth (Fig. 5)—and added scrap plastic hatches and hawser covers to the anchor winch housing (part No. 77). I

performed similar work on the afterdeck (Fig. 6) and extended the ventilators there by 3/16", made new tops for the ash chutes on the side of the hull from scrap plastic, filled the aft torpedo tube, and left the lip of the bow torpedo tube.

Finally I added small wire rings and eyes to the anchors, then attached fine chain from the rings of the two forward anchors through the hawseholes, around the capstans, and to the front of the anchor winch housing.

Superstructure. The superstructure is incorrect no matter which sister ship you build. Cut away all the "deck" between the upper deck and the bridge deck; leave only the outer 1/4" for the hammock berthing (Fig. 7).

Remove the aft 3/4" of the bridge deck to make room for the cage mast and wireless shack, then build the inner walls of the hammock berthings and install a new sheet styrene deck. The cross section (Fig. 8) shows part No. 12 through the hammock berthings. Fill the gun-mount holes in the tops of the hammock berthings: These weapons were removed in the 1910 refit. Be sure to remove all the cast-on rails from the superstructure.

Cut away the sides of the casemates (Nos. 27A and 27B) after cementing them to part No. 12. Also remove the corresponding hull sponsons to create a

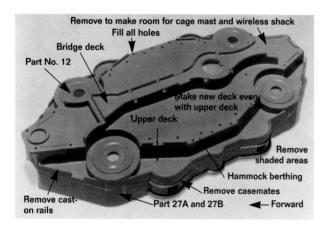

Fig. 7

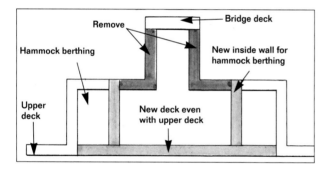

Fig. 8

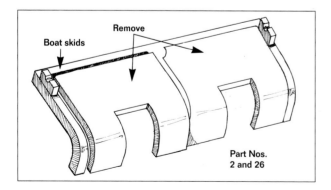

Fig. 9

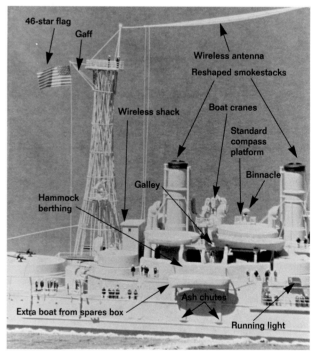

Fig. 10

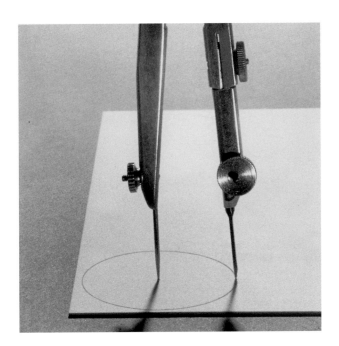

Fig. 11.

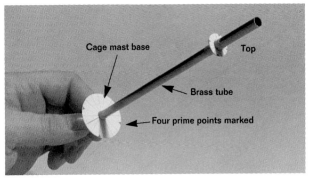

Fig. 12

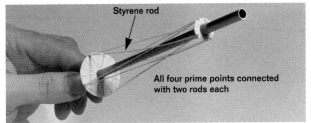

Fig. 14

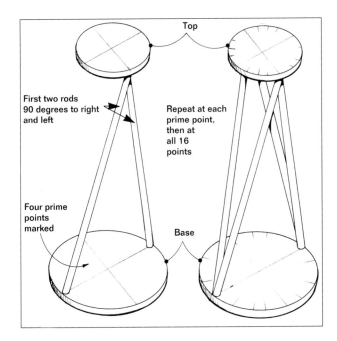

First two rods 90 degrees to right and left

Repeat at each prime point, then at all 16 points

Four prime points marked

Base

Top

Fig. 13

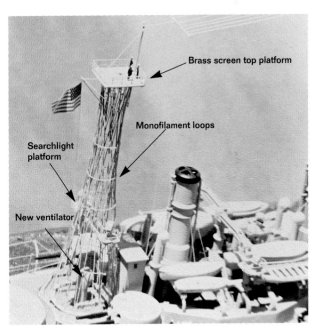

Brass screen top platform

Monofilament loops

Searchlight platform

New ventilator

Fig. 15

smooth surface on the sides of the ship. Next, glue the hull halves together along with the fore and after decks, then install the superstructure with its modified casemate sides and fill and sand the wide seams in the decks exposed by the modifications. Extend the ventilators (parts Nos. 24) that attach to the new deck with ⅞"-long styrene tubing. Extend the forward pair of ventilators (Nos. 54) ¼".

I built the wireless shack, the structure around the smokestacks, and a mid-deck galley from sheet styrene. The galley, which fits under the bridge deck, has outboard bulkheads about ½" out

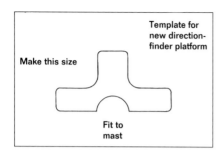

Make this size

Template for new direction-finder platform

Fit to mast

Fig. 16

from the bridge deck, with a roof that overhangs all sides.

Massachusetts lacked the covering on the boat skid; I modified part Nos. 2 and 26 (Fig. 9). Relocate the standard compass platform (No. 44) to the bridge deck between the stacks and install the binnacle only (No. 50) in its center. I fabricated sheet styrene emergency ration and vegetable lockers on the upper deck against the outer walls of the hammock berthings and on the bridge deck just forward of the wireless shack.

Now wrap .020" sheet styrene around the upper portions of the smokestacks so they resemble the stacks of the *Massachusetts,* then file the lower edge of each cap to produce a thin lip (Fig. 10). Remove all the cast-on pipes and ladders and add new ones of plastic rod and photoetched brass.

Cage mast. The cage mast looks daunting, but making it is easier than describing how. It's a hyperbolic structure made of straight rods connecting a base ring and a top platform. First use a cutting tool in a draftsman's compass to cut two circles from .030" sheet styrene (Fig. 11). The diameter of the base circle is 1 9/32" and the top one is 19/32".

Draw a line across each circle that passes through the center point, then draw another diameter 90 degrees from the first line.

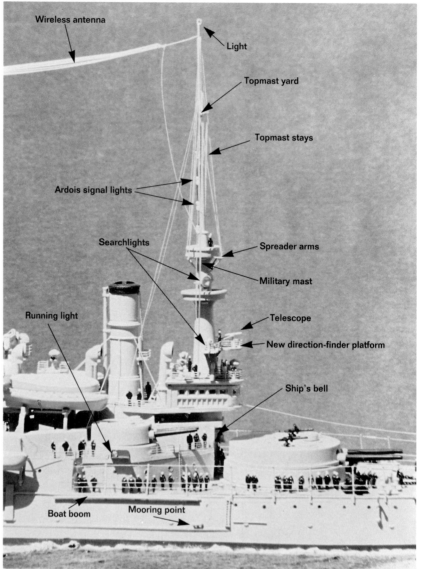

Wireless antenna

Light

Topmast yard

Topmast stays

Ardois signal lights

Searchlights

Spreader arms

Military mast

Running light

Telescope

New direction-finder platform

Ship's bell

Boat boom

Mooring point

Fig. 17

Next, bisect each quadrant, then bisect each segment again. You should have 16 points evenly spaced around each circle's circumference. Mark the four prime quadrant points (every 90 degrees) on the circumference for reference.

Score each circle 1/16" in from its outer edge to make the centers easy to remove later. Next, drill holes in their centers to install a brass tube. The tube keeps the base and top ring 4 15/16" apart, parallel to each other, and the four

prime points on each circle in line with each other (Fig. 12)

The structure is made of fine styrene rod; use either Evergreen .020" rod or the finest rod in the Contrail assortment. Starting with one of the four prime points on the small circle, attach two 5" lengths of rod, then attach the other ends on the large circle, 90 degrees to the left and right (Fig. 13). Repeat this process at the remaining three prime points (Fig. 14). Eventually, I attached two rods to each of the

16 points on each circle, each one going to a point 90 degrees to the left and right (Fig. 15).

Super glue loops of monofilament fishing line around the mast; be careful not to tie tight enough to distort the mast. Next, carefully cut away the center of both circles, leaving the rings.

I built the top platform and the searchlight platform from sheet styrene. The top platform is a frame holding a fine brass mesh deck. I used brass rod for the gaffholding, the flag, and the topmast. Photoetched ladders and rails add the fine details.

The cage mast rests on the rear of the upper deck just forward of the large aft gun turret. It surrounds a scratchbuilt ventilator. You may have extra searchlights in your spare parts box; I turned mine from PVC plastic on a lathe and added scrap plastic bases and details. Drill out the reflectors, and after painting them silver, add drops of 5-minute epoxy for the lenses.

Deck details. I extended the boat cranes to reach the upper deck on the superstructure, then detailed them with stretched-sprue cables.

Remove all the cupolas from the six gun turrets and fill the resulting holes with epoxy putty. Make new hatches and cupolas from sheet styrene and drill out all the gun barrels. Install two 3" guns (part No. 19) on top of each 13" turret, then omit the kit's other guns, which were removed in *Massachusetts'* 1910 refit.

On to the military mast: Discard the kit's direction-finder platform (No. 38), and make a new one from sheet styrene (Fig. 15). I added a scrap plastic telescope and searchlights, then installed brass rod spreader arms (under part No. 40) which accept the topmast stays. Replace the topmast and yard (No. 56) with brass rods and tubing so they support the rigging without bending (Fig. 17).

I used stretched sprue for all the rigging. I built the 10-wire wireless antenna flat on the workbench, then installed it between the masts. White glue simulates the insulators. I added clear glass beads for the Ardois signal lights and lantern on the topmast.

Most of the railings and ladders came from Gold Medal Models' photoetched brass set No. 350-4, but the main deck rails of *Massachusetts* were high, attached outboard of the deck. I made these stanchions with plastic rod and attached monofilament for the rails. I made new flag staffs for the bow and stern from brass wire and made their diagonal braces from stretched sprue.

I fashioned epoxy putty covers for the ship's boats, then added two more boats from my spares box, and installed a thin brass tube for the smokestack of the steam launch.

After all was painted and assembled, I added a 46-star flag, then filled the ports, bridge windows, and wireless shack windows with Kristal Klear.

To add life to a model, I add crew figures. My measurements showed the model to be larger than the kit's stated scale of 1/225. I calculated that the average sailor should be $5/16$" tall, and I obtained figures of that height from an architectural-model supply firm. With a little work and paint, they look great.

My base is particle board with walnut veneer edges and a walnut strip ledge to hold a Plexiglas case. Mix Celluclay with white glue to form the water in the diorama. Using a small screwdriver, form the wave pattern and wake before the material sets, then paint it with Floquil colors and coat it with acrylic gloss medium.

REFERENCES

• Alden, John D., *American Steel Navy*, Naval Institute Press, Annapolis, Maryland, 1972
• Coker, P. C., *Building Warship Models*, R. L. Bryan Co., Columbia, South Carolina, 1974
• Conway's *All the World's Fighting Ships 1860-1905*, Naval Institute Press, Annapolis, Maryland, 1979
• Davidson, Louis, *United States Battleships*, Waterline Shipmodelers Planbook Series, Pensacola, Florida, 1976
• Preston, Anthony, *Battleships of WWI*, Galahad Books, New York, 1972
• Reilly, John C. Jr., and Robert L. Scheima, *American Battleships 1886-1929*, Naval Institute Press, Annapolis, Maryland, 1980

SOURCES

• Contrail rod and tubing, available from Santos Models, P. O. Box 4062, Harrisburg, PA 17111
• Sheet, tube, and rod styrene: Evergreen Scale Models, 12808 N. E. 125th Way, Kirkland, WA 98034
• Photoetched details: Gold Medal Models, 12332 Chapman Ave., No. 81, Garden Grove, CA 92640
• Brass tubing: K&S Engineering, 6917 W. 59th St., Chicago, IL 60638
• Ship's flags: Model Expo Inc., P. O. Box 1000, Mount Pocono, PA 18344

WEATHERING AIRCRAFT MODELS WITH OIL PAINTS

Who says you're not an artist?

Fig. 1. Jon combines staining, blending, and dry-brushing to heavily weather this 1/72 scale LS Peggy. Photos by the author.

BY JON LOPEZ

All right. You're a modeler. But artists don't have exclusive rights to use oil paints. Top figure painters work with oils because the colors are easier to blend to produce subtle tones than enamels or acrylics. You can apply washes and dry-brush with oils, too.

I hope to dispel the notions that oil paints are expensive, hard to use, and slow-drying. And I'll show you how oils can be used effectively to simulate weathering on model airplanes. My techniques are staining (applying a wash), blending, and dry-brushing.

Materials. First select a finished model to experiment with. Make sure the model has a top coat of clear flat lacquer (such as Testor Dullcote) that will prevent the oils from affecting the color coats. My example here is a 1/72 scale LS Ki-67 Peggy made into a derelict, Fig. 2. My weathering included removing the "glass" areas and building an exposed internal structure for the rudder. Here is a list of materials you'll need:

• Oil paints in 1.25-fluid-ounce tubes. Raw umber and burnt umber are used often, but make sure you have a good selection of primary and secondary colors so

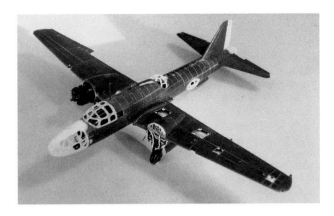

Fig. 2. Jon removed all the "glass" panels, one engine, and numerous panels from his model to achieve a derelict appearance.

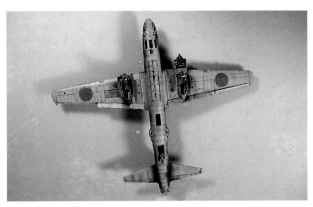

Fig. 3. Out of the sun and rain, the bottoms of abandoned aircraft weather comparatively little.

you can produce shades of the base colors that you used to paint the model.

• No. 6 square-tipped boar-bristle brush

• No. 1 sable brush with a pointed tip

• Plate-glass palette approximately 10" x 18" backed with a sheet of white paper

• Japan Dryer

• Paper towel

• Turpentine

A 1.25-ounce tube of oil paint will last many years, long enough to weather dozens of models. Look for oils in art supply stores and at national-franchise craft and houseware stores; often they're marked down to less than a dollar a tube. Sets of commonly used colors are also available, Fig. 4.

Stain. I call this a stain, but you may know it as a "wash." Begin by placing a few drops of Japan Dryer on the glass palette and tinting them with a touch of raw umber and burnt umber oils, Fig. 8. Japan Dryer accelerates the drying of oils. In this ratio of dryer to paint, oils dry in one to two minutes. (The dryer has a pink cast, but this disappears as it dries on the painted surface.)

With the point of the No. 1

brush, apply this stain to the recessed panel lines and rivet detail on the undersurfaces of the model. The flat lacquer coat will wick the

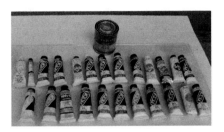

Fig. 4. Purchase an adequate selection of primary, secondary, and earth colors, along with a container of Japan Dryer.

Fig. 6. The stain is also good for adding realism to landing gear.

stain into the panel lines. Just touch the tip of the loaded brush to the surface, and zip!—a perfectly straight stain line. If you make a

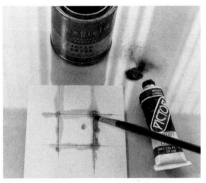

Fig. 5. Jon practices by applying his stain (a wash) on a sheet of scribed styrene.

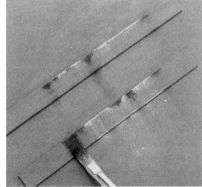

Fig. 7. Dry-brushing produces realistic weathering streaks and highlights the high points that would weather most.

Four shades of base color scrubbed into surface

Blend shades where they meet

Fig. 8. Blending

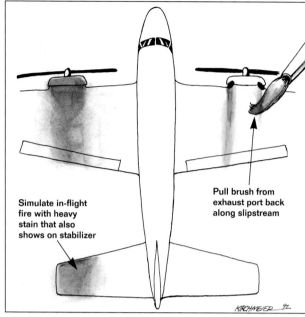

Simulate in-flight fire with heavy stain that also shows on stabilizer

Pull brush from exhaust port back along slipstream

Fig. 9. Exhaust and smoke stains

mistake, flush the area with dryer and then blot up the excess with a paper towel.

For darker lines, don't add more paint—just repeat the staining several times, allowing each application to dry. Stain the landing gear struts and wheels with a gray-green-brown mixture, Fig. 7.

Except for stains, the bottom surfaces of aircraft left out in the elements weather little. Abandoned Japanese planes found years later in the South Pacific islands had remarkably clean and fresh colors underneath, so don't overdo such surfaces. (Upper surfaces are, however, another story; see below.) Blending. When is a green object not green? When is a blue shade not blue? Objects that appear to be one color are in fact many shades, values, and tones of that color. The shape and texture of the surface, aging, wear, and fading produce these variations. The paint will also reflect the colors of objects around an aircraft. Thus, a model painted in a single

color looks unrealistic and toylike. Oil paints' ultrafine pigmentation makes models come alive with subtle color variations—a glaze of color over a painted undercoat.

To vary the color of the upper surfaces of my Japanese bomber, I mixed several lighter shades of greens, reds, and purples on my glass palette. The greens simulate the faded overall color; red represents the discolored areas of the hinomaru (the Japanese red-disk insignia)—and purple acts as the worn areas of the wing where the purple primer of the real airplane would show through after years of neglect.

Light at the top. Since the wings and upper fuselage receive more sunlight, the paint there fades. Thin the paint mixtures with dryer until they are almost transparent. Apply light green to one side of the square-tipped boar-bristle brush, then scrub the color into an area of the wing ¼" to ⅜" in diameter, Fig. 7. Now apply a second green color patch adjacent to

but not touching the first. Last, apply a third and a fourth shade of green next to them, then scrub them into the surface.

Now blend the colors where they meet. At these junctures the blending will create dozens of colors and shades, all green but no two alike. Perfect!

Stand at your workbench and keep the model at arm's length as you blend. You can see what you're doing and appreciate the process better. Now move along the wing, keeping the major color areas distinct. Don't repeat the colors in the same sequence, and make sure you vary the sizes of the color areas as you go. Scrub away!

I applied the same shades of green to the fuselage but concentrated the lightest shades on the spine. Scrub these colors into the surface, then drag them down the sides of the fuselage with the brush. If the airplane is a tail dragger, keep the streaks perpendicular to the ground, not to the center line of the fuselage. Water and

Fig. 10. The recessed panel lines and rivets on the plane's wing are accentuated with thinned oils.

weather affect the paint of an airplane similarly, bleaching and fading it from the top down, so the colors run like icing off a cake.

Dry-brushing. What is dry-brushing? How can you apply paint if the brush is dry? Well, almost dry. The idea is to lighten the points of a model that protrude from the surface: rivets, outside corners, hinges, and so forth. These areas wear and fade faster, and we can simulate these effects with paint.

In dry-brushing, apply a light color over a dark color to create streaks and to highlight certain details. Mix a light version of the base color and thin it with dryer. Pick up a little paint with the tip of the square-bristle brush and wipe nearly all the paint onto a rag. Swipe the brush over high points of the area you're detailing as if you're removing dust from the model.

Use several shades of tan and gray on the engines. To simulate exhaust stains on the wings, pull the brush from front to rear, Fig. 9. To represent the results of an engine fire, make the smoke stain carry all the way back to the horizontal stabilizer, following the airflow direction. Don't forget the fuselage sides and turret frames.

Whisk several shades of light base color down their sides.

Panel lines. After blending and dry-brushing, I accentuate panel lines on the top of the wing and fuselage with a mix of raw and burnt umber. Thin them with dryer and draw the panel lines on with the No. 1 sable brush, Fig. 10. You can also accentuate the cockpit by flooding this mix around and behind the details.

Overcoat. After you have completed weathering your model, set it aside to dry for a few days. Finally, overcoat the model with a clear semigloss lacquer to protect the finished product.

You can see that a model weathered with oil paints has more life to it than one painted in a single color. Even if you use only two colors for blending, the results will be noticeable. Make artist's oils the next addition to your toolbox!

SUPER GLOSS STRAIGHT FROM THE SPRAY CAN

Easy ways to achieve brilliant finishes

Pat used this Ertl 1/25 scale Super Nova to illustrate his easy-to-follow paint techniques—but he couldn't resist throwing in a few extra details! Robert Norris photo.

BY PAT COVERT

Runs! Drips! Dust! Orange peel! We've all experienced frustrating problems on the way to what we hoped would be an immaculate, "smooth-as-glass" paint job. These painting pitfalls can spoil an otherwise perfect model. The good news is that you can avoid problems if you simply understand why they occur.

Good body preparation, sound painting techniques, and proper finishing are the three main ingredients of a professional, first-class paint job. If you master these three phases of execution you'll get consistent, excellent results. To stick to the fundamentals, we'll discuss spray enamel. It's a good idea to master "the can" before working with an airbrush, because it's simpler.

Body preparation. Start with a good foundation. Body preparation is the most grueling—and boring—part of the painting process. It is also the foundation of every great paint job.

First, remove any molding seams left by the kit manufacturer. Examine the body carefully— some seams are almost unnoticeable. Lightly sand them off with 600-grit sandpaper; be careful not to alter any of the original body lines. Next, examine the body for sink marks. Fill these with body putty or, if they are small, with super glue.

In fact, super glue works well as a filler on small applications. It dries quicker than putty and it's great for pits and panel lines. It doesn't work well on larger areas where contouring is necessary because it can't be shaped like putty. It's tougher to sand, too.

Use a sanding block to reduce and contour body panels. Rough sand with 240- to 300-grit sandpaper, and use 400- to 600-grit for the final sanding before priming.

Priming. Priming gives the surface a "tooth" to which top coats can adhere, and it protects the plastic from being melted or etched by "hot" paints such as lacquer. Priming also helps you spot flaws in the body. When you see a glitch in your body work, repair it, sand it smooth, then re-prime the area. My favorite primer is Plast-I-Kote Spot Filler and Primer, available at K mart. This quick-drying primer is thicker than the average spray primer. It fills pinholes and scratches, so you'll need fewer finish coats.

After you have worked out the problems in your body work, Fig. 2, spray on a final coat of primer. Allow it to harden overnight. Then wet sand with 800- to 1,000-grit wet/dry, Fig. 3. A smooth primed surface helps prevent "orange peel" (a bumpy or dimpled surface) when the top coats are applied.

Don't sand roughly during this step: You don't want to expose the plastic. Sometimes it's hard to gauge your progress while wet sanding, so stop and dry the body occasionally to check for areas you may have missed.

Pat doesn't start anything he can't finish—and what a finish! (Above) "Candy Man," Ertl's '49 Ford. (Below) Monogram's '56 T-Bird, mounted on a shortened Ertl Chevelle chassis.

Priming, sanding, re-priming, and resanding are tedious but necessary. Paint doesn't cover up mistakes—it makes them bigger. The goal is to achieve an ultra-smooth prime surface: Once you've done so, you're ready to paint!

Controlling the environment. Here's a corollary of Murphy's Law: "If there is one speck of dust in the air, it will land on the middle of your roof." You can't eliminate every bit of dust in the air, but a clean, well-ventilated room certainly helps. A fan-ventilated spray booth, besides protecting you and the room, shelters the car body between paint coats. I use a

simple cardboard box, but you can improve on that by using a booth to control dust and fumes.

Paint doesn't flow well at temperatures lower than 67 degrees F. You'll get a heavily textured or "orange peel" finish. Another environmental problem is high humidity. Moisture in the air can mix with the paint as it is sprayed, causing pits and clumps in the finish. If it's raining, don't paint!

Spraying technique. Before spraying, mount the body and parts securely. Attach the body to the top of a tall spray can: 2¾" diameter works well for most vehicles. Secure the car under the

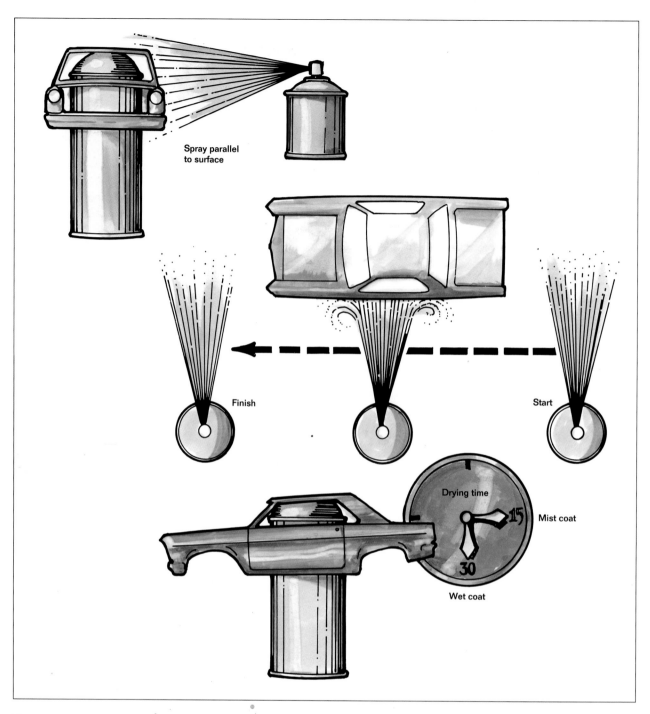

Fig. 1

roof and on the sides with masking tape. Mount body parts such as the hood and trunk lid on top of ⅛" or ¼" styrene rod: Put a drop of super glue on the end of the rod and attach it to the underside of the part, Fig. 4. Mounting the part in this way gives you a "handle" so you can hold the part in one hand and the spray can in the other.

Warm the paint so it flows easily when sprayed. Run hot tap water 2" deep into a baking pan, Fig. 5, and put the can in the water for a few minutes until it's warm. Now you're ready to spray. Master the following techniques for consistent results:

• Stroke—Start your spray off the surface and follow through until you have cleared the surface again, Fig. 1. Never start spraying directly on the model, and never stop in the middle. Runs and drips can result.

• Angle—Keep the nozzle and sweep of your stroke parallel to

Fig. 2. The final primer coat. All the wrinkles—except the secret one inside the wheel well—have been worked out.

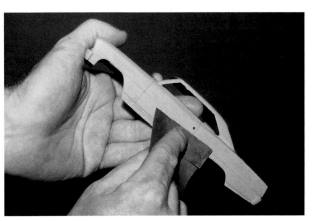

Fig. 3. Let the primer cure for at least a day, longer if you live in a humid climate. Then wet sand it with fine-grit paper.

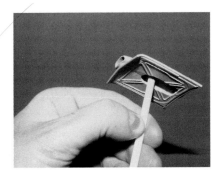

Fig. 4. Super glue small parts to styrene rod for easy painting.

the surface, to avoid paint buildup, drips, or runs.

• Sequence—Spray one panel at a time. Develop a sequence: For instance, right side, left side, front end, rear end, and top. Don't forget to include the hood and trunk in each sequence so all parts receive equal coverage.

• Distance—For a uniform layer of paint, hold the can a consistent distance from the subject. For mist coats, hold the can about 9" from the surface; for wet coats, about 7".

• Drying time—Allow ample time between coats. Otherwise, paint may drip or run. Wait 10 to 15 minutes between mist coats, 25 to 30 minutes between wet coats.

Begin with mist coats—light coats that give the surface a "tooth" to which wet coats can adhere. Don't try for complete coverage in one or two coats. You'll usually need three or four mist coats. Remember, wait 10 to 15 minutes between coats.

After your mist coats have completely covered the surface, apply the wet coats, Fig. 6. Thicker than mist coats, these are applied at a closer range. Lay down just enough paint for consistent, wet coverage. It's better to apply a wet coat in several quick, light strokes than to risk laying down one heavy coat. Proceed cautiously, and check coverage after each stroke. Stay with your sequence. Again, wait 25 to 30

Fig. 5. Warm paint flows better. Pour hot tap water in a baking pan and let the cans warm for a few minutes.

Fig. 6. No fancy mount needed: Tape the car body to the top of a spray can.

Fig. 9. The first round of paint sanding dulls the finish, but don't be alarmed—the shine will return as you continue sanding with finer grits.

minutes before starting to apply the next coat.

The wet coats required vary with the brand of paint. Glossy model paints tend to be thick, so three or four coats should do. Thinner spray paints, such as Krylon, require more coats.

Finishing with two coats of clear enamel gives the paint depth. Several years ago I stumbled upon an interesting technique that smooths out ripples. Immediately after applying the final wet color coat, apply a top coat of clear enamel. The clear mixes with the final color coat and magically smooths the surface.

However, clear enamel has a yellowish cast that darkens with age. Don't use it over white paint

or any color you think may be soured by such a tint.

Final finish: super gloss. If you've followed the game plan so far, you should have an acceptable paint job. But even the best out-of-the-can results can be improved by rubbing and waxing, so why not go the extra mile? A polishing kit and wax are all you need for a mirror-like shine.

I've tried both Micro Mesh, Fig. 7, and Millennium 2000 polishing kits. Both yield exceptional results. Each kit contains several sanding-cloth grits, a foam sanding block, a bottle of polish, and a polishing cloth. These polishing systems work well on most paints except acrylics, which tend to be too soft.

Before you begin buffing, make absolutely sure the paint is dry. (Remember: Wait a week to 10 days.) Sand the paint with one of the coarser grits supplied in the kit. (If your paint job is smooth, skip the 1,800 and 2,400 grits. Start with 3,600 grit and work up from there.) Wrap the sanding cloths around the sanding block. Always use straight, back-and-forth strokes—never a circular motion. Use the sanding cloths either wet or dry; dry if you're a beginner, because it's easier to gauge your progress. You'll notice that the first grit dulls the paint, Fig. 8. Don't worry—the succeeding grits polish and restore the luster.

Beware of sharp creases and edges on the body, especially with coarse grits: Too much sanding pressure can grind right through the paint and expose the primer, or even the plastic. Go slow and check your progress often; shiny areas are an obvious clue that you've missed a spot. After you've completely dulled the finish, move to the next-finer grit and repeat the process.

Each time you move to a finer grit, be sure to remove scratches left by the previous sanding. You'll start appreciating your efforts when the 8,000 grit begins returning shine to the paint. The 12,000 grit increases the luster but still leaves a slight haze.

Applying the kit-supplied polish eliminates this haze and brings

Fig. 10. Model wax adds luster, protects the paint, and goes on quickly. Buffing is a cinch—it's as easy as shining your shoes!

out the gloss. Wrap the polishing cloth around the foam sanding block, add a drop or two of polish, and buff a body panel, Fig. 9. Once you've covered the panel with polish, buff with a dry portion of the cloth until all the compound has been removed. The results are astounding! The polishing compound produces a brilliant gloss. You'll wonder, "Does it get any better than this?"

It does! Wax increases the finish's luster and depth, and it protects the surface, too. The Final Detail model wax, Fig. 10, is easy to use. Apply the wax with a soft cloth. I recommend white flannel, available at any fabric store. It's the same material supplied with the polishing kit, and it's inexpensive. You can buy it by the yard.

Cover your index finger with the cloth, dab on a bit of wax, and rub the wax onto a panel using small, circular strokes. After covering the panel, buff off excess wax with a dry portion of the cloth, then move through your finishing sequence. All that's left now is to sit back, admire your great work, and pat yourself on the back for your outstanding effort!

Following these preparation, application, and finishing methods will produce a super gloss every time—but it takes practice. If you doubt a certain technique, try it on a junker or scrap plastic before you tackle your pet project. Good luck, and may your next finish be a first place finish!

SOURCES

• Micro Mesh polishing kit: LMG Enterprises, 1627 S. 26th St., Sheboygan, WI 53081
• Millennium 2000 polishing system: MSC Model Products, 22 S. Balsam St., Lakewood, CO 80226
• The Final Detail model wax: Treatment Products Ltd., 3057 N. Rockwell St., Chicago, IL 60618

MODELING A '49 MERCURY

Easy tips for beating up a beater

Fig. 1. Not every car model has to look showroom shiny and new. Tom's Ertl/AMT '49 Mercury is done up as a restorable relic.

BY TOM LAMARRE

FOR SALE: 1949 Mercury Club Coupe, good transportation, good muffler, $50.00. Today it's a collector's item, but in the early 1960s a '49 Merc was usually a "beater," a well-worn car that did not look like much but still had some miles left in it. Newspapers had plenty of ads for these semi-junkers for sale for less than $100.00. The subject of this chapter is a typical transportation special, the kind of car that sat in the back row of a '60s used car lot.

Fig. 2. Rust showing through the paint is a typical problem with old cars.

Fig. 3. Old cars are often missing sections of chrome trim. A sharp knife and sandpaper are all you need to remove trim strips molded on model car bodies.

Fig. 4. Use a hot knife, soldering gun, or candle flame to soften the plastic enough to create this rotted-through look.

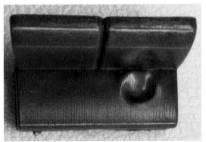

Fig. 5, left. Surface rust is typical of an old, weathered car. Sanding through the gray paint exposes the brown undercoat, producing a realistic surface rust effect.

Fig. 6. Heat applied to the seat cushion softens the plastic to simulate broken springs underneath the fabric.

AMT/Ertl's 1/25 scale '49 Mercury is a rugged tank itself, having been issued in various forms since 1963. A few simple weathering techniques will help the Merc show its age.

Crusty body. The first step is to remove some of the body's chrome—the trim strips aren't chromed in the kit but are molded on the body. Parking lot damage or rusted retaining clips took their toll on the "protective" chrome; it was usually the first thing to go. I shaved the trim from the door with a sharp hobby knife, being careful to leave the adjacent sections intact, then finished with progressively finer grades of sandpaper, Fig. 3. After painting the model, I applied small dots of flat black paint to simulate the holes for the retaining clips. When trim parts company with a real car, a ghostly outline of the missing piece usually remains. Years of accumulated dirt and wax leave a permanent discoloration on the paint. Use a pencil or fine-tip felt pen and a straightedge to create the outline of the missing trim on the model.

Rusty paint. There are two kinds of rust found on old cars: surface rust from worn or chipped paint, and rusted-out, eaten-away metal. Rust-out often occurred behind the wheel openings of old Mercs. I use a hot knife to simulate rust-out (available from Mailcorp, 413 Eynon St., Scranton, PA 18504). You could also use a candle or match flame held close to the area you want to damage, but be sure you don't ignite the plastic. Styrene fumes are toxic! Shape jagged edges while the plastic is still soft, Fig. 4.

Use a different technique for surface rust. First, apply a coat of flat brown paint (I use Testor's No. 1186), followed by the final color coat. Some of the popular '49 Mercury colors were black, dark green, gray, and burgundy. Rust shows up best against light-colored paint, so I used flat gray (Testor's No. 1163). Gloss paint would be inappropriate for an old, weathered car.

When the color coat is dry, lightly sand the finish to reveal the brown undercoat—instant rust! Vary the depth of sanding for a more realistic effect. Concentrate surface rust on the hood, trunk, tops of the fenders, edges of the roof—wherever sun, rain, and snow would wear the paint and expose bare metal, Fig. 5.

Another junker idea is to paint the hood, one door, or fender a different color (flat black, for example) to simulate replacement parts obtained at a junkyard.

Because chrome oxidizes over the years, use chrome or silver paint instead of metal foil for the remaining trim. The kit's plated parts (bumpers, taillight housings, and headlight rings) should also be toned down with paint. Either chrome paint or a clear flat overcoat will do the job.

Dusty interior. My old Merc is beat up on the inside, too. I heated the plastic and indented the driver's seat cushion to simulate a sagged cushion caused by broken springs, Fig. 6. Most Mercs had a gray mohair interior, so after a coat of flat gray, I applied a flat black wash for grime, concentrating on the rear shelf, floorboards, and dashboard. Uneven sanding on the top of the dashboard produced a faded, splotchy appearance.

Paint the engine and chassis flat brown, the universal dusty, rusty shade seen under the hoods of old cars. Coil fine wire around a section of the tail pipe to recreate a do-it-yourself repair job.

No owner would buy whitewalls for a rusty relic, and be sure to scruff and sand the tread and sidewalls until they look like old weathered rubber. Only covered wheels are included in the kit, but a missing wheel cover would be a nice touch. Scrounge a bare wheel from your spare parts box.

Gone are the days when shiny new Mercs cruised the streets, but once in a while an unrestored car fresh out of a barn turns up at a swap meet. Usually there's a For Sale sign in the back window and a crowd surrounding the car. After all, one man's junker is another man's jewel.

MODELING A
FORD GT 40 IN 1/24 SCALE

Modifying Fujimi's 1966 LeMans winners

BY GREG KOLASA

Time flies: It's hard to believe it was 27 years ago that Ford's GT 40 was dominating the racing scene, winning Le Mans, Sebring, and Daytona in 1966. I longed to return to those wonderful years by modeling the GT 40s.

Fujimi offers the 1966 Le Mans 1-2-3 finish in its 1/24 scale Historic Cars series (kit Nos. 12101, 12102, 12103). Revell repackaged the Fujimi kits and dressed them in 1966 Sebring and Daytona racing trim (kit Nos. 7130 and 7131). Revell dropped

The Ken Miles–Lloyd Ruby car (No. 98), winner of Daytona in 1966, was an early GT 40 Mk. II. In the same year at Sebring, Dan Gurney's Mk. IIA (No. 2) came close to winning but was disqualified when Gurney tried to push it across the finish line.

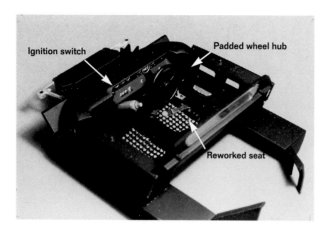

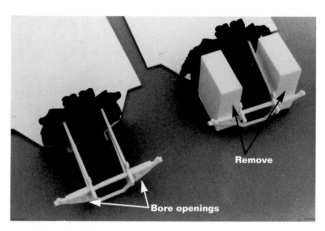

Fig. 1. Greg drilled out the vent holes in the seats. He also rearranged the control switches and padded the steering wheel.

Fig. 2. They're the rule at Le Mans, but the "suitcases" are excess baggage on American racers.

the kits after 1990, but you can still find them around—and since the markings are simple, you can customize decals to model the same racers.

Because the model cars are made from the same molds, they don't have the differences that made each GT 40 unique. That's a small problem—I'll show you how to build and finish the GT 40 of your choice.

Wheel and tires. The kit's magnesium wheels are realistically plated with a dull aluminum finish. Paint the center section of the wheels flat gray, leave the rim plated, and paint the knockoff spinners metallic gray to set them off from the rest of the wheel.

Here's where the similarities among the cars' wheels end. I spray painted No. 98's wheels gold. After painting a thin blue line around the outside sidewalls, I applied Goodyear decals and finished the sidewalls with Testor's Dullcote.

Interior improvements. No fancy color schemes here—almost everything is flat black.

I painted the pedals, trim, switches, and fuel-cell access panels silver. The fire extinguisher is

red, and the seats and steering-wheel rim are black semigloss.

It was tedious, but I enhanced the seat ventilation holes by gently drilling each vent hole. This scrapes black paint away from the hole, and the resulting white ring replicates the metal grommets found on the real seats, Fig. 3.

I eliminated two switches from the center console and replaced the speedometer on the far left side with a large ignition cutoff switch, Fig. 1.

Unlike the kit-supplied steering wheel, Mk. II wheels had a large, padded hub. I chucked a 1/8"-diameter plastic dowel in a drill and ground the end to a slightly convex shape. I sliced off a 1/16" segment, glued it to the steering-wheel hub, and painted it black semigloss, Fig. 1.

At the rear. Le Mans rules required the cars to have room for two people and their luggage. Fujimi's molding included suitcases as part of the chassis; to model an American racer, we must remove them, Fig. 2. Cut off the top, then the bottoms of the tab where the rear cross member mounts.

That's the easy part. Unfortunately, the far-rear cross member

is molded to the suitcases: Carefully cut away the suitcases, leaving only the cross member. The openings in the cross member must be opened up, too.

Complete the rear-end assembly according to the instructions, including paint. Minor exceptions to the kit's paint scheme include flat-gray exhaust pipes, and painting front and rear suspension members slightly different shades of silver.

Individualizing No. 98. A few simple modifications will give the cars their true identity.

Car No. 98, driven by Ken Miles and Lloyd Ruby, won the 1966 Daytona race. Later that year Miles was at the wheel of the same car, repainted light blue and wearing No. 1, as it finished second at Le Mans.

Fujimi's molding includes the rear-deck "snorkel" scoops seen on the Le Mans Fords, but at Daytona, No. 98 didn't have these scoops, Fig. 3. Remove them and their bases, fill gaps with epoxy putty, and sand smooth, Fig. 4. Another molding that should be removed from this particular car is the bulge in the roof, designed to give the driver more headroom. Be

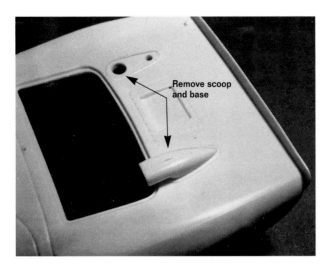

Fig. 3. The winner of Daytona was an early Mk. II without snorkel scoops.

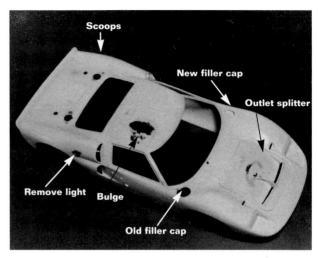

Fig. 4. Moving exterior details around leaves gaps; fill holes with putty and sand them smooth. Greg made the radiator outlet splitter from sheet styrene.

careful not to damage any surrounding details.

The fuel filler cap is on the wrong side. Its location was determined by which side would face the pit crew in a given race; it belongs on the left side of No. 98. I filled the original filler port, drilled a new one in a corresponding location on the left side, and installed a scrap of sheet styrene in the new port for the kit filler cap to rest on, Fig. 4. To correct the shape of the radiator outlet splitter, Fig. 4, I built a new one from sheet styrene. I used the kit-

supplied divider as a template to get the proper curve. Leave off the photoetched vanes that the kit places at the edges of the hood.

Remove the two molded number-illumination lights located forward of the rear wheel cutout, Fig. 4. Cut carefully. You'll need to reuse them. Install one of the rear deck to match the molded one on the right side, Fig. 5.

The kit supplies photoetched hood pins but early Mk. IIs such as No. 98 had turn-style latches; I made these from sheet styrene. There is a hood pin in the center of

the rear cowl; I added a fastening wire that runs to a screw located between the roof vents, Fig. 5. The kit provides a clear center scoop for the rear deck; I painted this scoop white.

The upper "shoulder" intakes should be divided horizontally, Fig. 6. I made this divider from sheet styrene.

The jack hooks supplied for the kit's front grille looked too deep to suit me. I trimmed them to match my photos of the car, Fig. 7.

Before installing the clear headlight covers, paint the inside

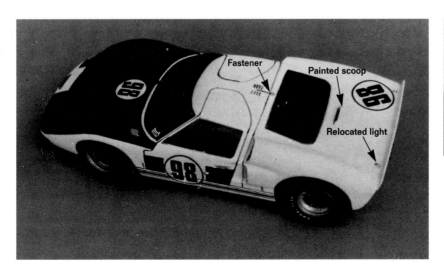

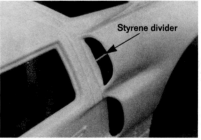

Fig. 5, left. Details, details: The kit-supplied rear-deck scoop is clear—paint it.

Fig. 6. Photo research revealed this intake detail. A styrene divider does the trick.

Piano wire

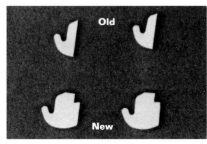

Fig. 7. The jack hooks didn't look right to Greg; he trimmed them to his taste.

Fig. 8, left. Does stretching the body onto the chassis make you nervous? a piano-wire body stretcher helps.

of the headlight buckets flat black, including the shelves that the covers rest on. While the flat black paint is out, paint the rest of the inside of the body shell so you won't see unpainted plastic when the car is viewed from a low angle.

The body fits tightly on the chassis, and it's an even tighter fit with my fat fingers in the way! I found a cure for that how-far-can-I stretch-this-before-it-snaps anxiety: I formed a 6" segment of piano wire into a V, bent the last ½" at a right angle, and used this tool to stretch the lower panels while slipping the body onto the chassis, Fig. 8.

The GT 40 door handles resembled large rocker switches: You depressed the forward edge with your thumb, and the rear section popped out of the body to form a grab handle. However, both cars I was modeling had a loop welded on the driver's door handle to allow quicker operation. I drilled two holes in the handle and made the U-shaped attachment with wire, Fig. 9.

GT 40 Mk. IIA. Revell kit No. 7131 depicts the car that almost won Sebring in 1966. The Mk. IIA driven by Dan Gurney and Jerry Grant broke down minutes from the finish. (An open-topped GT

40 driven by Miles and Ruby won).

As with No. 98, several minor improvements make No. 2 a better replica. Again, the roof bulge has to be modified. Instead of the molded teardrop shape, the bulge should be circular, Fig. 9. It's easiest to replace the entire molding. You can use any material you like to get the correct shape—I used the nose of a large radar pod from Monogram's 1/72 scale P-82 Twin Mustang. The dome on the real car was pop riveted over the hole in the roof, so there should be a seam where the bulge meets the roof.

On this car, the two carburetor inlets on the engine cover were

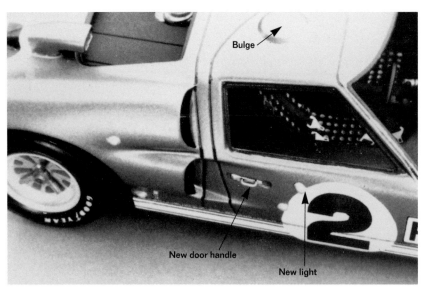

Bulge

New door handle

New light

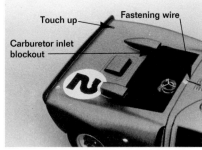

Touch up

Fastening wire

Carburetor inlet blockout

Fig. 9, left. Now it's Dan Gurney's turn: The roof bulge was added to accommodate drivers that rode tall in the saddle of the 40"-tall Ford.

Fig. 10. You know you're a serious modeler when you add somebody else's touch-up.

blanked off. I closed these openings with sheet styrene, painted aluminum, Fig. 10.

Other minor improvements included dividing the shoulder scoops and adding a grab handle on the driver's door, same as on No. 98. Also, I added two more number-identification lights: one on the driver's door, at 11 o'clock on the number; and one on the passenger side number, at 2 o'clock. See Fig. 9.

Several details that I changed for No. 98 also work for No. 2: The fuel filler cap stays in the same spot; the snorkel scoops remain; the radiator outlet splitter is the right shape; and the jack hooks on the front are the right size. As on car No. 98, I painted most of the interior and inside of the body flat black.

Painting. These tips apply to both cars. Painting the back of brake- and parking-light lenses red gives the realistic look of a transparent colored lens. I painted the cowl latches and the screw slots in the tail spoiler silver, then gave them a thin flat-black wash to pick out details. The back of the roof vents are painted dark gray. I outlined the door and cowl seams with India ink.

Both cars were painted with gloss colors (also an accurate color on street versions). I finished with Testor's Dullcote: It tones down the shine, enhances the dullness of flat-painted areas, and coats the decals.

Custom decals. The GT 40s were sponsored almost solely by Ford and were devoid of the clutter trademarks seen on most racers. In fact, the name, "Ford" didn't even appear on the cars until later in 1966 at Le Mans. The only exceptions are the Autolite stickers.

Fig. 11. Greg combined kit decals with Super Scale trim film to make his number disks.

Car No. 98 wore fluorescent-red identification patches on the nose and left door. The kit supplies orange decals; I painted red patches instead. This car's rocker-panel stripes were dark blue, but the kit decals were black. I marked and painted the decals before applying them.

The Revell decals were a bit thick. I loaded No. 98's decals with solvent, but on No. 2 I replaced the white number disks with Super Scale decal trim film, Fig. 11. (A variety of solid-colored sheets is available, allowing you to customized decals to fit any car.) After applying the number disks I trimmed the numbers from the kit decals and applied them to the disks. I had painted the small part of the "2" that falls over the rear-deck scoop, Fig. 10.

Final lap. Photos show car No. 2 with protective covers taped over the lights. I got the same look simply by painting the clear covers white and replicating the tape with strips of white decal.

I secured car No. 2's front cowl with the kit-supplied hood pins. I left off the twin vanes on the front hood, same as car No. 98, and painted No. 2's front-cowl hinges bright silver (they're flat black on the other car). Since the number-illumination light was

deleted from the left side of the real car, I hand painted a slight blemish to represent a touch-up in that spot, Fig. 8. Finally, I attached wire to the rear-cowl hood pin.

All in the family. By now you've probably noticed that I have a special place in my heart for all variants of Ford's GT 40. Although the Revell kits are no longer available, Fujimi's three GT 40s give you a good start on modeling these famous Fords. Photo references, innovative decaling, painting— and this article—will help you model your favorites.

THE FORD GT 40

From the mid-1950s through 1962 Ferrari dominated the 24-hour Le Mans endurance race. However, in 1962 Henry Ford II announced that Ford Motor Co. wanted to race, and that it was withdrawing from the US Automobile Manufacturer's Association's 1957 self-imposed ban on racing.

After an unsuccessful bid to buy Ferrari, Ford contracted the Englishmen Roy Lunn, Eric Broadley, and John Wyer to accomplish the next best thing—to beat Ferrari at Le Mans. Broadley's Lola GT provided a starting point for the new British division

Dave Friedman photos courtesy of Ed Sexton, Revell/Monogram

of Ford, Ford Advanced Vehicles (FAV), in Slough England. The result of FAV's work was the Ford GT 40, so named because it was 40" tall.

Early prototypes struggled with undependable gearboxes and a disturbing tendency to leave the ground at high speeds. The GT 40 was negatively consistent in 1964—eight starts netted eight DNFs (Did Not Finish). The designers returned to the drawing board, the builders set up shop near Dearborn, Michigan, and they produced the Mk. II.

With new gearboxes, improved aerodynamics, and 7-liter 427 engines, the Mk. II began to gain on Ferrari. Further refinements resulted in the Mk. IIA—a world-class contender that heralded Ford's new dominance.

In the cars pictured here, No. 98, a Mk. II driven by Ken Miles and Lloyd Ruby, won the 1966 Daytona. And Dan Gurney's Mk. IIA came so close to winning the 1966 Sebring that when the blue No. 2's engine failed he tried to push it across the finish line (he was disqualified). But Ford's greatest victory of 1966—and the culmination of the Ford GT program—was the 1-2-3 finish at Le Mans, which included the former No. 98m painted light blue and wearing No. 1.

Ironically, both cars were wrecked in a late-night pile-up at the 1967 Le Mans.

REFERENCES

• Archibald, Steve, *Ford GT 40 Sports Cars*, Sapphire Publications, Hemel Hempstead, Hertsfordshire, England, 1984.
• Jones, Gordon, and John Allen, *The Ford That Beat Ferrari: A Racing History of the GT 40*, Kimberly Publishers, London, 1985.
•Spain, Ronnie, *GT 40: An Individual History and Race Record*, Osprey Publishing, London, 1986.

SOURCES

• Sheet styrene: Evergreen Scale Models, 12808 NE 125th Way, Kirkland, WA 98034

• Decal trim film: Super Scale International, 2211 Mouton Dr., Carson City, NV 89706

DETAILING A
1966 SHELBY GT350H

The Rent-a-Racer goes from driveway to display case

BY GREG KOLASA

I had first-rate reference material when I set out to detail Monogram's 1/24 scale 1966 Shelby GT350H—the real thing in my driveway. But even then I had to work my way up through some of the other 60s Shelbys, including a kitbashed version of a 1/43 scale GT350. At last, when Monogram came out with its current series of 1/24 GT350s, the man and the model met.

Three Monogram 350s are available; the 1966 GT350H I have modified as No. 1900 is a remake of the 1965 GT350. I used Monogram's 1966 GT350 (third issue) for No. 1012. This chapter describes the changes required to enhance the details on a "from the box" GT350H in order to depict two specific cars as well as to explain some of the more subtle

Fig. 1, top. Monogram's 1/24 scale series inspired Greg's models of the "Rent-a-Racers" he and his fiancee own. Three-quarters of Hertz Shelbys were black and gold, the rest red, green, white, or blue.

Fig. 2. Those not fortunate enough to own a real Shelby GT350H can accurize their engine compartments by getting in touch with the Shelby American Auto Club.

changes between early and late production Shelbys.

The two cars I have modeled are SFM6S1012—for Shelby Ford Mustang, 1966, Street version 1,012th consecutive unit—and SFM6S1900, the 1,900th GT350 built. Both are GT350H versions delivered to Hertz in Ohio. (The 1012 went to Akron in February 1966, and 1900 west to Dayton in April of the same year.) The GT350Hs were interspersed with standard non-Hertz GT350s on the production line, and they were not given serial numbers to indicate Hertz or non-Hertz status: You can't tell from a serial number whether the car was originally a rental.

I own the real 1900, and it represents what about 800 of the 1,000 Hertz car batch looked like: black and gold with chrome "Magnum 500" wheels. Carol Padden, my fiancee, owns the 1012, one of the "other color" cars. Originally red, it was delivered without the wide top stripes, referred to as either "rally" or "LeMans" stripes, as were a handful of non-black cars. It came equipped with the special master cylinder referred to in the instructions and known as the Minnesota Automotive (or MICO) "piggyback" master cylinder.

We believe that the 1012 was delivered with the chrome "Magnum 500" flywheels, but today it wears the aluminum "10 spokes," and that's how I modeled it. Notice that since the 1012 was to be painted red, I used the body parts from the 1966 GT350 kit, molded in white. The GT350H kit is molded in black. That's why some of the photos show white and black parts.

Wheels. Since cast-aluminum wheels aren't an option on the GT350H kit, I resin cast a set of the aluminum wheels using Monogram's 1/24 scale Boss 429 "10 spokes" option as patterns (kit No. 2854). Cement the wheels to the bottom of a container slightly higher than the depth of the wheels. (Use rubber cement, since you'll want to remove the wheels.) Mount the wheels with the detail side up (Fig. 3). Spray a light coat of WD-40 lubricant spray oil on the bottom of the container and wheels. Next mix a batch of Dow-Corning JRTV silicone rubber. JRTV, a two-part compound that's much like body filler, is usually mixed by adding the hardener until you've achieved a specified color. Pour the goop

Fig. 3

Fig. 4

into the mold and allow it to cure. Air bubbles will rise to the surface.

When the rubber has cured, remove the chunk of JRTV from the container and simply pop the wheels out of the mold. Place the mold in the bottom of a coffee can with a string tied to the open mouth of the can (Fig. 4). Mix a small batch of fiberglass resin and pour it into the cavities in the mold. Then before the resin sets, swing the can a few times in an arc; the centrifugal force generated by the rotation pulls the resin down into the wheel cavities.

Allow the resin to set for a few minutes to a few hours, depending on how much hardener you use; now you can pop the wheels out of the mold. Some slight filing or sanding may be needed on the backs of the wheels, but the result should be virtually indistinguishable from the injection-molded original.

I painted the 10-spoke aluminums with bright silver lug nuts, but I left the Magnum chromes with black pockets, silver lugs, and gold-and-red center caps. I picked up the "Goodyear" lettering left over from a 1/43 scale Ford GT40 kit of mine.

The body. I first filled the five circular openings in the radiator support; they don't exist on the 1012, the 1900, or any other GT350. Next you can begin work on the engine room, although most detailing will be done after you paint the body.

Remove the cylindrical object forward of the driver's side shock tower, then fill and sand the engine compartment wall (Fig. 5). (You can use the top of this device to simulate the heater blower motor, which the kit doesn't provide.) Next, drill two small heater hose holes just inboard of the blower motor. Also drill holes for the choke cable and the fuel inlet. Fill small sink marks on the tops of the fenders. You should sand the "MUSTANG" and "289" emblems off the fenders (Fig. 6); Shelbys didn't have them.

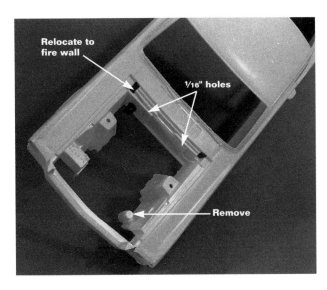

Fig. 5

Fig. 6

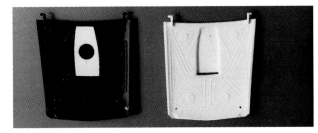

Fig. 7

Drill a ⅛" hole in the sculpted body cutout under where the side scoops mount (Fig. 6). This hole (3" on the full-size car) ducts cool air from the side scoop to the rear brakes for cooling. All '66 Shelbys have these functional side scoops. A mold seam near the rear quarter windows should be sanded out; then you can put the body aside until you're ready to prime and paint.

The last two body-related items are the rear valance panel and the hood. The 1012 has no backup lights, so fill the holes for mounting them and sand the area smooth. The hood supplied with the kit represents the fiberglass top/steel frame unit used on the GT350 from mid-1965 onward.

The 1900 has an all-steel hood, and to simulate this, cut a piece of thin sheet plastic and install it in the bottom of the scoop opening (Fig. 7). The scale 9" hole simulates the appearance of the all-steel hood, which was nothing more than a standard steel Mustang hood with a steel scoop welded to the top. The 9" hole allowed fresh air into the engine compartment. Finish by drilling out the holes for the hood lock pins.

Engine. The High Performance Ford 289-cubic-inch V-8 (or more commonly, the HiPo 289) comes complete with the Borg-Warner T-10 4-speed transmission. Although the shift rods are molded into the case, they are visible. If you highlight them with silver paint, they simulate the real things well. Details you can add include fuel pump and lines (from

Fig. 9

Fig. 8

body to pump and from pump to carburetor), ignition coil, plug wires, heater hoses, lower radiator hose (only the upper one is supplied with the kit), PCV hose, oil breather cap hose, choke cable-and dipstick. I just scrounged through my spares box and picked out bits of scrap metal to simulate these smaller details.

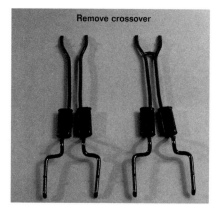

Remove crossover

Fig. 10

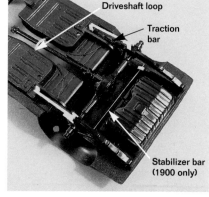

Driveshaft loop

Traction bar

Stabilizer bar (1900 only)

Fig. 11

Both of these automobiles carry "Cobra" steel scattershields in place of the standard cast aluminum bell housings—paint the 1012's steel colored, the 1900's black. Paint the transmissions black with aluminum-colored tail-shaft housings and engine; use gloss blue on the engine blocks. The 1012 has early-type bare aluminum valve covers with polished fins and lettering; the 1900's are wrinkle-finish black with bare aluminum fins and lettering.

The oil pans (Fig. 8) require a bit of work, too. If assembled as included in the kit, the bottom portion of the "T" not only mounts off-center, but when viewed from

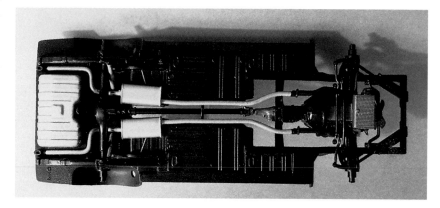

Fig. 12

the top, it's also hollow. This problem is easily remedied if you cement a thin piece of sheet plastic to the top of the "T" before mounting it to the body of the pan. Then delete the alignment pins and glue the halves together. The oil pans on both cars, as well as the fuel pump and intake manifolds, are aluminum; the pan and the intake have blue bolts.

The carburetors are gold, and the air filter elements are white. I hand-painted the "Autolite spark plugs" and "289 cubic inches" decals for the top of the air cleaner, since they're not provided in the kit. Leave the spark plug wires off until you mount the engines into the chassis (Fig. 9): This way you won't have to handle the engine with the fragile wires exposed. Secure the plug wires with Krazy Glue; yes, I installed mine in the correct 1-5-4-2-6-3-7-8 firing sequence. Your engines are now complete; set them aside until you're ready to install them.

Undercarriage. Detailing the undercarriage is not a big job. Most of the details found on the real GT350 are reproduced in the kit, the notable exception being

the underside traction bars (Fig. 10) found on 1966 Shelbys from number 0800 or so on. I fashioned the spring clip plate mounts from thin sheet plastic and the bars themselves from 1/16" plastic-coated (cementable) wire. Note that the forward end of the bar mounts just ahead of the spring forward mount.

The 1012 and the 1900 exhaust systems both dispense with the "crossover" pipe just aft of the transmission cross member so I removed it (Fig. 11). The only other addition is the rear stabilizer bar on the 1900. It's similar to the bar used on the 1969 Shelbys and Mustang Mach; I fabricated it from thin piano wire. Small blocks of plastic mount the center of the bar to the frame rails, as on the real 1900, and I made the spring clip plate mounts from sheet plastic as well.

Drill two 3" (scale) holes into the rear wheel wells—they are the air outlets for cooling the rear brakes. You'll need a driveshaft safety loop, too; I made mine from thin sheet plastic. It bolts to the front inboard seat belt anchor bolts—both cars have it.

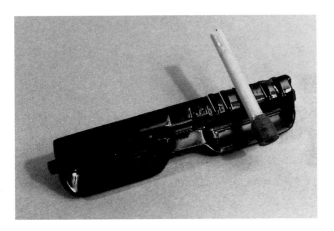

Fig. 13

Fig. 14

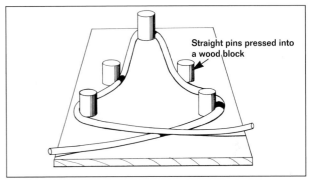

Straight pins pressed into a wood block

Fig. 15

Fig. 16

Paint the entire undercarriage semigloss black as on the real cars. The fuel tank and the exhaust pipes are silver (natural metal). The last 4" (scale) of the tail pipes are flat black. All rear-axle-related items are semigloss black also, although the shock absorbers are orange. Paint the inside of the wheel wells flat black.

Interior. As with the undercarriage, all the pertinent details are here, and the only real changes at this point are to add small items. I added the choke and fresh air vent knobs to the bottom of the dashboard; likewise with the parking brake handle. The steering wheel provided with the kit accurately copies the real thing, and the only change needed is to drill out the spoke holes. The 1012 carries the optional real wood steering wheel (the standard 1966 wheel is plastic wood); the one supplied with the 1965 Shelby GT350 is the same type. (The only problem: My 1965 GT350 is now missing a steering wheel!)

I simulated the courtesy lights in the rear inside quarter panels with small-diameter tubing cut into short lengths and cemented in place. These are silver with white lenses. I used scrap plastic to extend the steering column down to the floor (Fig. 13), and I fashioned the turn indicator stalks from wire.

The kit comes without seat belts. All '66 Shelbys came with 3" competition seat belts in front and standard 2" Ford belts in the rear. The front belts (Fig. 14) were made from wire, cardboard, and flat black ⅛"-wide drafting tape. I made a jig—straight pins pressed into a wood block (Fig. 15)—to facilitate fabrication of the buckles. I simply threaded the wire between the pins, pulled tight, and removed it from the jig. The result is eight identical buckles. A drop of epoxy on the buckles closes off the center

Fig. 17

Fig. 18

Fig. 19

section as on the actual ones. I also added the release handle to the inboard seat belts.

All 1965 and 1966 Shelbys came with black interiors. I sprayed the whole unit semigloss black, then painted the carpets flat black and the driver's side floor mat gloss black. The rear seat fold-down sections have been trimmed with chrome, so I painted them silver. Dashboards are semigloss black, and the glove door and gauge housing on 1012 are flat black. The 1900 carries the optional woodgrain (plastic also) trim on the bezel and on the glove door.

The 1012 carries the brake warning decal above the radio. ("This vehicle is equipped with competition brakes. Heavier than normal brake pedal pressure is required.") The 1900's is below (Fig. 16). It's a gold decal with black lettering; ditto for the owner-installed GT350H dashboard plaque on the glove box door (1900 only). The armrest bases, the door panel trim, and the door handles/window cranks are silver.

Both cars have banded (top tinted) windshields; I painted the tinted area with Testor's transparent blue before installing them in the body. The interiors are now complete (Fig. 17).

Body paint. Testor's Red (No. 1204) is very close to the '66 Ford Candy Apple Red that 1012 is painted, and Testor's Gloss Black is used for 1900. Each car has six coats of paint, wet sanded with 600 paper between coats. This step provides a smooth paint job without any out-of-scale "orange peel." My 1012 was modeled without the gold LeMans stripes (Fig. 18). Even though my real car has them now, within the next few years it'll be repainted without the top stripes, the way it was delivered to Hertz in 1966.

The LeMans stripes on the 1900 are Testor's Gold; Scotch foggy translucent Mending Tape

provides a nice sharp edge. The stripes on the actual cars were not constant width, and in 1/24 scale, the difference in widths is almost too small to model. (If they had been a constant width, they would have appeared to widen at the front edge of the hood.) I used the decal side stripes from the kit.

Install the windshields and rear windows and paint the headliners flat black. In order to hide the windshield edge, sun visors cut from flat stock were cemented in.

Paint the window trim silver and the engine compartments on both cars semigloss black; then mate the bodies to the chassis as per kit instructions. Note that the side scoop area on the body is semigloss black on all color cars except, of course, the black ones.

Install side scoops, quarter windows, and radio antennas on the front fenders. I added the aluminum "GT350" nameplate to the right rear face panel. Install bumpers, taillights, headlights, and front and rear valance panels per kit instructions. I made the Hertz Sports Car Club front license plates on the real cars and on the models.

Engine compartment final. Detail the radiator support by adding the protruding supports to locate the hood pins to the front of the support. Snap the hood into place, and hold the radiator support in place while you mark the location of the hood pin supports.

Cut the supports from sheet stock; then, with the hood in place, drill through the holes you drilled earlier and through the supports. Then epoxy straight pins in place from the underside (again, with the hood and radiator support in place on the body) so the pins protrude through the top of the hood. Trim them to the right length. This serves both as a detail

Fig. 20

Fig. 21

touch and as a way to locate the hood fore and aft while in the closed position (the hinges are loose).

Install the radiator and paint the support assembly semigloss black to match the engine compartment. The hood pins are silver; the voltage regulator is blue with yellow "Autolite" lettering. The core of the radiator is flat black and the cap is silver. Cut the small white service specifications decal on the top edge of the support from scrap stock.

The real 1012 had evidence of "DS0 291" chalked on the radiator support; this was a Ford code for the District Special Order number, and it pertained to what region of the country the car was delivered to. I painted this white.

Drill a shallow hole in the lower corner of the radiator to locate the lower radiator hose. Sand the two protruding blocks (presumably from the molding process) from the back of the grille and paint it flat black with silver bars on the front. I left the trim around the front bottom chrome and picked out the vertical bars on the running horse emblem with red, white, and blue.

Touch up the sun visors with flat black; then assemble the interiors into the bodies. (Don't forget the rearview mirrors, provided with the kit, and be sure to clean the fingerprints on the inside of the windshield and rear windows.)

Final assembly of the engine compartment is next. I scratchbuilt the "piggyback" master cylinder fitted to some of the Hertz cars (including the 1012) from bits and pieces in my scrap box and installed it. The standard unit was used on 1900. I changed the 1900's battery to a Motorcraft type; this involved making filler cap bars from sheet stock. The battery is white with a red top and white cap bars. I painted

the 1012's Autolite "Sta Ful" battery black and used the Autolite decals provided with the kit (Fig. 20).

Speaking of decals, a couple of homemade additions are called for: the white "battery OK" decal above the starting solenoid, the silver service specifications decal on the shock tower, the Shelby IO plate on the front fender lip, and the "GT 350" badge on the rear face panel. I cut these from silver decal sheet; the lettering was painted in black.

Other additions include the inner-fender-to-fuel pump fuel line, choke cable, heater hoses, and lower radiator hose (all from Display Scale). Install the radiator support and grille; cement the upper radiator hose in place; install the Monte Carlo Bar, export brace, and windshield washer bag (all provided in the kit); and add a piece of scrap plastic to simulate the starting solenoid to the inner fender just aft of the battery.

As a last touch in the engine compartment, I picked out the fender and grille support bolt heads (actually, painted them in, for there aren't any) in silver. I added the hood latch spike and hook to the bottom of the 1900's hood (1012 uses only the hood pins to keep the hood closed), and drilled two pin holes into the front of the radiator support to install a hood prop (Fig. 21).

Install side scoops (using Krazy Glue), front and rear bumpers, wheels side-view mirrors, and radio antennas.

These conversions consist of a large number of subtle additions, any one of which might not make a lot of difference. But add them all up, and the result is two super models of Hertz' amazing rent-a-racers.

The Raciest Rental Ever. Hertz Rent-a-Car's Shelby GT350H may have been the fastest thing

The Hertz Shelby GT350H: neglected for years, now available only for ransom.

ever from the rental lot. In 1965 Hertz was approached by the makers of the new Shelby GT350 with a proposal that Hertz buy a limited number of the new auto. Hertz saw Shelby American's bet and raised it considerably, increasing the initial order of 200 to 1,000. About 75 percent of the GT350s produced for Hertz in the 1966 model year were black and gold—a scheme based on actual Hertz models built in the 1920s.

Mechanically a twin of the GT350, the GT350H soon suffered unexpected abuse: Stories abound of cars returned with blown engines or carpeting burned when welding roll bars for a weekend of racing. The idea lasted only one year—Hertz reportedly lost money on the deal—but today the aura of legend surrounds the GT350H.

Shelby American was the brainchild of Carroll Shelby—Texan, fast talker, and fast driver (winner of the 1959 LeMans race, among others). His partnership with Ford Motor Company in the early '60s produced first the classic Shelby Cobra, then, after the introduction of the Mustang in 1964, the Shelby Mustang GT350. Shelby claimed this custom Mustang 2+2 could do 0–60 in 5.7 seconds and 0–100 in 14.9, top speed 133 mph. Mating that power to world-class suspension and handling, the Shelby GT350 was a sports/racing machine unlike anything seen previously in this country.

REFERENCES

• Kopec, Richard J., *Shelby American Guide,* published by the Shelby American Automobile Club (SAAC), P. O. Box 681, Sharon, CT 06069
• *Mustang Recognition Guide,*

3816 Industry Blvd., Lakeland, FL 33811
• Shelby American World Registry and Issue 52 of the *Shelby American Magazine:* SAAC, above

SOURCES

• Radiator/heater hoses, spark plug wire: Mailcorp, 413 Eynon St., Scranton, PA 18504
• License plate and mud flap (used on 1900) photo etchings:

Detail Master, P. O. Box 1465, Sterling, VA 20167
• I/16" tubing: Plastruct, 1020 S. Wallace Pl., City of Industry, CA 91748

DETAILING RADIAL ENGINES

Improving kit engines for 1/48 scale aircraft

Figs. 1 and 2. Aircraft with radial engines are perfect subjects for superdetailing. Bob's 1/48 scale Otaki F4U-1A Corsair received a new engine from a Monogram P-61 (Left) A close-up of the new engine shows the ignition harness ring and modified distributors added to the P-61 version of the Pratt & Whitney R-2800.

BY BOB STEINBRUNN

Few things evoke the essence of aviation as much as the noisy, smelly, smoked fire-belching, oil dripping, ear-splitting radial aircraft engine. Jets and turbines lack the character of a radial. Liquid-cooled engines, buried in the airframe, are out of sight and out of mind—it's hard to relate to something you can't see. Radials, however, are right up front and exposed by open cowlings.

Starting a radial engine is far more complex than the pushbutton simplicity of a turbine. Properly manipulating the mixture lever, throttle boost pump, and starter is an art requiring an experienced pilot. You've accomplished something when the radial coughs and spits, pops, and sputters, then settles down to a steady, throaty roar. It makes a fellow grin to get one lit off on the first try.

Because the radial engine captures what I enjoy most about aviation, it's one of my favorite assemblies to model. Model aircraft engines in 1/48 scale range from superb miniatures to ludicrous blobs of plastic. This chapter will help you radial lovers make accurate engines to complement your favorite aircraft.

Fig. 3. Williams Brothers' 1/8 scale Wright Whirlwind kit is an excellent reference source for superdetailing smaller scale engines.

Fig. 4. Another Williams Brothers kit is the 1/8 scale Pratt & Whitney R-1340 Wasp engine.

Getting to know the beast. First, study the radial engine. Knowing the shapes and terminology of engine parts helps to produce an accurate, detailed replica. I examine and photograph real radials at air shows, but some are closely cowled and prevent examination of their rear areas. If this is a problem for you, or you don't live near an airport, the next best thing is to acquire one of the excellent Williams Brothers 1/8 scale model engine kits.

Williams Brothers offers the LeRhone rotary Wright J-5 Whirlwind, Fig. 3, and my favorite, the Pratt & Whitney R-1340 Wasp, Fig. 4. These kits are intended for the advanced builder, but with a bit of care you should be able to assemble one fairly easily. A large-scale engine kit such as this provides a challenging break from routine modeling as well as an interesting weekend. Most important it gives you a better understanding of the components of a radial. I built one as a training exercise—a large-scale

version of the detail I would later add to my 1/48 scale engines.

A better engine. I start with the best kit engine I can find. Table 1 furnishes my recommendations for 1/48 scale engines. Many old kits (and some recent ones) provide only the front face of a radial engine and many of the details are missing. For example, Otaki's (now Arii) Corsair features a poor representation of the 18-cylinder Pratt & Whitney R-2800 Double Asp engine 100000.

Monogram's P-61 kit has a dandy. Some modification of Monogram's engine is necessary to represent the variant in the Corsair, but you're ahead of the game with the better engine.

If you have the wherewithal, copy the engines using RTV molds and casking resin, rather than robbing one kit to re-engine another. I like to have photos of the particular engine I'm modelling since different versions of the same model engine vary greatly in appearance. Good references are old editions of *Jane's All The World's Aircraft*, which feature a section on aircraft engines.

To remove molded-in engine faceplates, drill holes around the perimeter of the engine, then cut from hole to hole with a sharp blade, Fig. 5. A half-round file will clean up the cowling interior.

Next, fabricate the engine fire wall out of sturdy sheet styrene cut to the size of the inside diameter of the cowling. Locate the fire wall so the engine nose case protrudes the correct distance from the cowl.

Now, I know we've thrown out the old engine and brought in a better one, but there's more. This

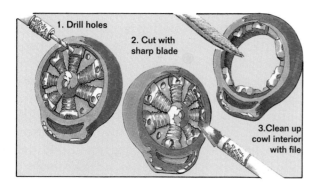

1. Drill holes

2. Cut with sharp blade

3. Clean up cowl interior with file

Fig. 5. Removing molded-in engine

Fig. 6. Bob carefully removed most of the molded-in detail from the 1/48 scale version of the R-1340 Wasp from Monogram's T-6 Texan kit.

TABLE 1: ENGINE REPLACEMENTS

ENGINE	APPLICATION	RECOMMENDED SOURCE (1/48 SCALE)
WRIGHT R-1820 Cyclone 9 cylinder, single row	B-17, SBD, F2A, FM-2	Monogram B-17, Tamiya F2A
Pratt & Whitney R-1830 Twin Wasp 14 cylinder, twin row	P-35, P-36, B-24, C-47, TBD, F4F	Monogram TBD
Wright R-2600 Cyclone 14 cylinder, twin row	B-25, TBF, SB2C, A-20, A6M Zero[1]	Revell B-25[2] Lindberg TBF[3]
Pratt & Whitney R-2800 Double Wasp 18 cylinder, twin row	F4U, F6F, F7F, F8F, B-26, A-26, P-47, P-61	Monogram P-61[4]

NOTES
1. For early Tamiya Zero and Rufe, use Tamiya engine case on Revell B-25 engine.
2. Although undersize, Revell's engine works well in closely cowled Japanese aircraft.
3. Lindberg's engine works best in Monogram TBF
4. One Monogram P-61 engine is molded complete, the other front row only.

may sound drastic, but cut and file off all molded-on detail, Fig. 6, including valve pushrod guides, spark plugs, wiring, ignition harness ring, and propeller governor. Preserve as much cooling gill detail as you can during this operation. The details you'll add will be more petite scale-like, three-dimensional, and will vastly improve the appearance of your engine.

Next, drill out the prop hub and crankcase to accept 1" lengths of K&S Brass tubing, Figs. 7 and

8. This tubing comes in many diameters and as displayed in a rack at most hobby shops. Choose two consecutive sizes; one will fit inside the other and act as a sleeve bearing. This setup allows you to finish the propeller separately, makes it removable to prevent damage when transporting the models and, best of all, allows the propeller to spin freely.

Using Fig. 11 as a guide and your photos for references, replace the detail you removed. I use

Fig. 7. The P-61 engine again, this time in a Monogram P-47. Superdetailing is easily seen in a 1/48 scale model.

Fig. 8. The engine from Revell's 1/48 scale B-25 was used to improve the old Tamiya Rufe.

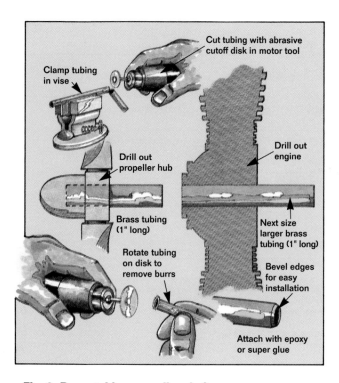

Fig. 9. Brass tubing propeller shaft

Clamp tubing in vise

Cut tubing with abrasive cutoff disk in motor tool

Drill out propeller hub

Drill out engine

Brass tubing (1" long)

Next size larger brass tubing (1" long)

Rotate tubing on disk to remove burrs

Bevel edges for easy installation

Attach with epoxy or super glue

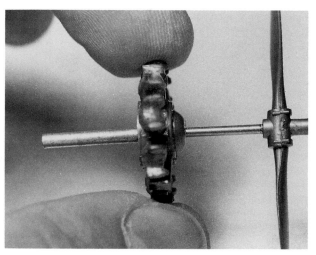

Fig. 10. Consecutive sizes of 1"-long brass tubing makes it easy to remove the propeller and allows it to spin freely.

stretched sprue solder wire, and thin plastic rod for these details. To make detailing easier, start at the rear of the engine and work your way forward. Exhaust stacks and the collector rings are usually behind the engine and can be made from solder with the ends hollowed out.

Some engines have valve housing and inter-cylinder oil drain lines, Fig. 12, so study photos of the engine you're detailing to see if they are present. Next come spark plugs, valve trunnion caps, oil sump plug, and pushrod housing seats. Attaching these small parts is easier if you first drill shallow holes with a pin vise and a No. 77 drill, then cement

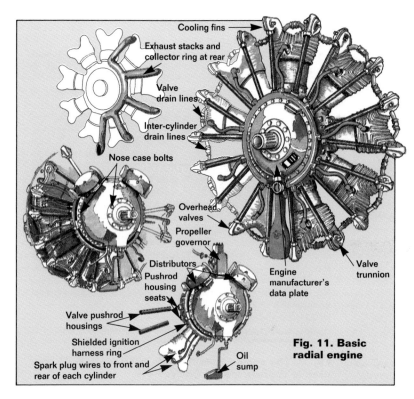

Cooling fins

Exhaust stacks and collector ring at rear

Valve drain lines

Inter-cylinder drain lines

Nose case bolts

Overhead valves

Propeller governor

Distributors

Pushrod housing seats

Engine manufacturer's data plate

Valve trunnion

Valve pushrod housings

Shielded ignition harness ring

Spark plug wires to front and rear of each cylinder

Oil sump

Fig. 11. Basic radial engine

TABLE 2: ENGINE COLORS

Crankcase, oil sump, gear or nose case	Medium gray
Cylinders	Aluminum or black
Ignition ring and spark plugs	Aluminum
Ignition wires	Black
Pushrod housings	Black or aluminum
Exhaust stacks and collector ring	Rusty brown
Intake manifolds	Black
Propeller governor	Black

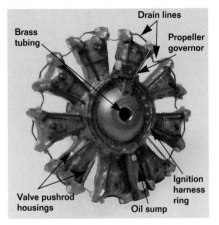

Brass tubing

Drain lines

Propeller governor

Valve pushrod housings

Oil sump

Ignition harness ring

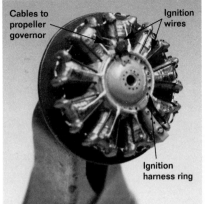

Cables to propeller governor

Ignition wires

Ignition harness ring

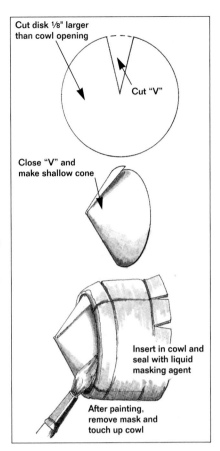

Cut disk ⅛" larger than cowl opening

Cut "V"

Close "V" and make shallow cone

Insert in cowl and seal with liquid masking agent

After painting, remove mask and touch up cowl

Fig. 14. Masking engines

Fig. 12, left. Stretched sprue, plastic rod, and sheet styrene replace the details on the T-6 engine. Note the oil drain lines.

Fig. 13. Painting is done and the ignition harness ring and wires are installed.

them with white glue applied with a small paintbrush.

Using sheet styrene, manufacture the oil sump pump and propeller governor. If necessary, modify the distributors or magnetos. The R2800 engine from the Monogram P-61 kit has oval distributors, fine for the P-61 and P-47 but not for the version in the Hellcat and Corsair. Their distributors are cylindrical, and can be scratchbuilt from sprue or plastic rod.

Painting the mill. This is the best time to paint the engine. Table 2 is a general guide if you lack other suitable reference. I find Testor's No. 1138 gloss gray a close match for crankcase gray. Cowling interiors were usually natural metal or painted zinc chromate, but there were many exceptions.

Add a manufacturer's information plate made from silver decal trim film painted with black lines to the crankcase or oil sump. Or use a manufacturer's plate included with Waldron Products' photoetched "Radio front panels and cockpit data plates."

After the paint is dry, add the valve pushrod guide tubes from the crankcase to the top of the

cylinder. Stretched sprue or plastic rod with a constant diameter is ideal here. Next come the ignition wiring and harness ring usually found on the front of the engine. Wires run out of the ring to the spark plugs, one to the front and one to the back of each cylinder. I like to use thin wire unwound from an electric motor armature.

Paint the pushrods and wiring next, then touch up mistakes, Fig. 13. After everything is dry, check the fit of the engine in the cowling and slide the propeller into place. Doing this now will reveal fit or clearance problems while they are still easy to fix.

If you must paint the model after the engine is installed, here's an easy way to prevent overspray. Cut a disk from paper approximately ⅛" larger in diameter than the cowl's opening, Fig. 10. Cut out a "V," then make a cone by closing the "V." Insert it into the cowl; seal the edges and slit with liquid masking agent or white glue.

After painting and overcoating, remove the cone and touch up the cowl edges. Now slide the propeller shaft into the hole in the crankcase, and you're done.

REFERENCES

• Gunston, Bill, *World Encyclopedia of Aero Engines*, Patrick Stephens Limited, Wellingborough, England, 1986
• *Jane's All the World's Aircraft 1945/6* (reprint), Arco Publishing Co., New York, 1977

SOURCES

• Sheet, tube, and rod styrene: Evergreen Scale Models, 12808 N. E. 125th Way, Kirkland, WA 98034
• Brass tubing: K&S Engineering, 6917 W. 59th, Chicago, IL 60638
• Photoetched detail parts: Waldron Model Products, P. O. Box 431, Merlin, OR 97532

MODELING THE LEGENDARY B-17F FLYING FORTRESS IN 1/48 SCALE

Converting and detailing Monogram's B-17G

The B-17F was the fastest version of the Flying Fortress. Paul's conversion uses the classic Monogram B-17G kit. Most of the conversion deals with the shape and armament of the nose—B-17F nose armament varied widely, so Paul duplicated one specific airframe. The "Wabash Cannonball" decal comes from Microscale (now Super Scale).

BY PAUL BUDZIK

I built my first Monogram 1/48 scale B-17G when it was newly released, and I still consider it an excellent kit. Ten odd years later, after countless viewings of Memphis Belle, Twelve O'Clock High, and The War Lover, I finally gathered enough inspiration to convert another kit to a B-17F. True, Revell issued a 1/48 scale) F-model, but I feel Monogram's kit is superior and a better starting point for an accurate replica. Monogram's interior detailing is more complete, the wings and engines are better, and the fuselage modifications would not be difficult.

Out of the box, Monogram's kit is an early B-17G with unstaggered waist gunners' positions and no Cheyenne tail turret. These characteristics were typical for B-17Fs, too, so the conversion didn't require major surgery. The most obvious differences between the two types were the G's "chin" turret, "cheek" gun blisters, and more blunt nose transparency. Nose armament of the B-17G was improved in response to head-on attacks by defending Luftwaffe fighters. There were other minor differences, and I made detail improvements to the Monogram classic as well.

Forward fuselage modifications. The first part of the project was removing the chin turret. I cut away the turret fairing and filled the resulting hole with .080" sheet styrene (Fig. 1). To get the plastic to blend in with the cylindrical fuselage, I placed the styrene on a glass jar about the same diameter of the fuselage and put it in a toaster oven set at 400

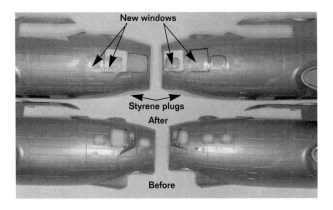

Fig. 1

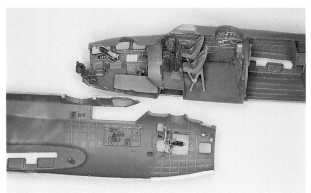

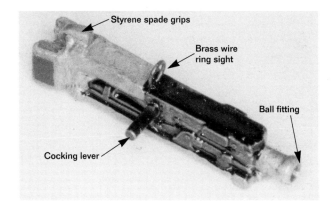

Fig. 2

Fig. 3

degrees. The heat softened the plastic, which then draped over the bottle.

After the plastic cooled, I placed it against the fuselage and traced the opening onto the new piece. After repeated cutting and trial fitting, I cemented it in place. Let the plug protrude slightly so it can be blended in with the contours of the fuselage with sandpaper. Time spent accurately fitting and cementing will save a lot of filling later.

The next step was to alter the cheek windows. Nose armament and window configuration on B-17Fs varied widely, but the mid-production F that I wanted to model had large, flush windows mounting the .50-caliber machine guns in positions opposite those on the Monogram kit. To make the changes, I cut away the window areas on both halves of the fuselage and replaced them with sheet styrene and 1/12" clear acrylic sheet formed over the glass jar in the toaster oven.

The oversize acrylic pieces were cemented in place, then sanded to blend with the fuselage contour. I painted the edges of the clear parts black in case they could be seen on the finished model. The final outline of the windows can be established later by masks and paint. This window method eliminates both the optical distortion of injection molded windows and the gaps around the windows themselves.

The kit cockpit detail was good, so I didn't add much. I filled the hole for the pin that supported the chin turret and removed the base for the turret control yoke. I added a rack with three oxygen bottles to the right side of the bombardier's compartment (Fig. 2), altered the ammo box arrangement, and built a new support for the bombsight from .015" sheet styrene. I used a bombsight from a Monogram B-25 kit (also found in the B-26 and B-29 kits).

I modified the hand-held .50s by adding different spade grips made of styrene along with ring sights and cocking levers fashioned from brass wire (Fig. 3). New barrels for the guns were cut from brass wire. I machined brass ball fittings to the nose guns. The ball fittings allowed the gun to be aimed without letting in the frigid outside air. I bored holes in the end of the balls to accept the barrels added after painting the model.

The trickiest part of the nose was installing the guns and ammo feed belts. I needed to attach the nose cone to complete the contouring of the fuselage and windows. This meant that everything had to be inside, yet I didn't want any gun barrels protruding to hamper finishing. This was the reason for the ball fittings. I drilled holes in the cheek windows, then cemented the gun receivers in place along with flexible ammo feed chutes made from strips of soft metal.

The nose cone and gun mount were another story. The Monogram nose is too stubby for an "F" so I made a mold from dental acrylic resin (see "Casting parts in dental acrylic resin," September

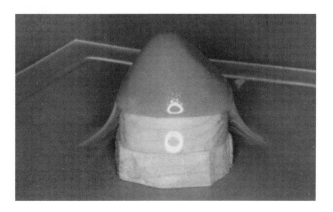

Fig. 4

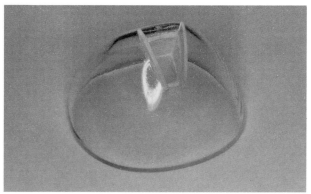

Fig. 5

1989 *FineScale Modeler* magazine) and vacuum formed a new nose from 1/32" clear acrylic (Fig. 4). I cut an opening for the gun mount, boxed it in with acrylic scraps that I milled to a thin cross section (Fig. 5), then drilled a hole to accept the ball mount.

The real aircraft had an internal rod framework that supported the gun mount. To simulate this, I cemented a scrap piece of olive drab styrene to the edge of the nose cone (Fig. 6), then drilled holes in

Fig. 6

the extension to accept .020" brass wire bent in the shape of the gun supports (Fig. 7). After painting the support rods olive drab, I cemented them in place with super glue. Next, I added an ammo feed belt and bent it so it would reach the ammo box when the nose cone was attached to the fuselage. After the fuselage halves were joined, I then cemented the nose cone in place and sanded it flush with the fuselage. Next, I cemented the kit windshield in place and machined a new astrocompass blister from clear acrylic.

Rear fuselage improvements. There's a gap between the radio compartment floor and the fuselage sides, so I added sides to the assembly from the floor to the first complete horizontal rib on the fuselage (Fig. 8). I removed the molded-in oxygen hose from the fuselage side and the radio operator's table and filled the hole in the floor. A new tabletop was made from sheet styrene and a radio from a hunk of acrylic. I added two auxiliary crew seats by modifying additional pilot seats.

Fig. 7

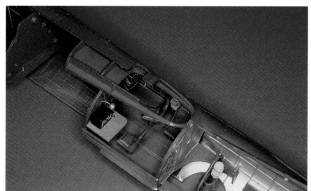

Fig. 8

Fig. 9

Fig. 10

Fig. 11

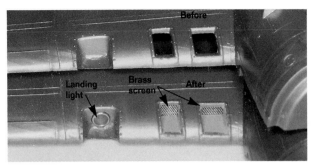

Fig. 12

Fig. 13

Fig. 14

I had to fit a roof to the compartment to separate it from the cabin fairing and to provide an attachment point for the machine gun mount. I made a cutout for the hatch in the roof and added vertical supports and a forward bulkhead.

The kit fuselage opening for the radio compartment hatch was uneven, so I enlarged it, lined it with sheet styrene, and cut a new opening (Fig. 9).

Monogram's G kit has fixed waist windows, but the F has removable panels. To display them open, I added a small strip of styrene to the top of each opening and small fillets to the lower corners (Fig. 10).

I added sheet styrene floorboards and brass tube gun mounts to the waist positions. Then I sanded the entire fuselage smooth and rescribed all panel lines. I sanded and polished all clear sections with plastic polish (available from plastic suppliers) to eliminate scratches. Then I reestablished the slightly raised panels under the cockpit windows with .010" sheet styrene. After they were cemented to place I sanded them down further. I engraved a depression for the wind deflector just forward of the radio compartment, fabricated a new deflector from sheet brass, and cemented it in place in the open position (Fig. 11).

Wing improvements. Before I cemented the wing halves together I wanted to enhance the appearance of the leading edge vents. I first eliminated flash, then used sheet styrene to box in and square the sides and tops of the openings from inside. I cemented pieces of No. 80 brass screen to the inside face of the

Fig. 15

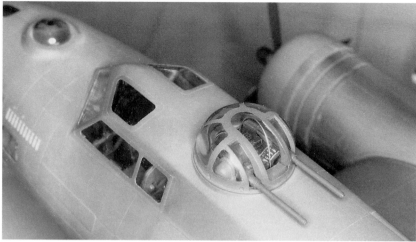

Fig. 16

Fig. 17

Fig. 18

vents with heavy gap-filling super glue, being careful to keep the glue from plugging the screen (Fig. 12). I drilled out the landing lights and replaced them with shaped acrylic rod with aluminum tubing bezels.

I didn't cement the landing gear struts in at this time, but I installed their mounting plates—the struts go in after painting. For better fit of the wing halves I removed flash and adjusted the mating surfaces, which included thinning the trailing edges. I cemented the halves while using masking tape to position the nacelles and the leading edge. The trailing edge was held together in a two-piece wood jig (Fig. 13) that kept the wing flat and straight. I filled and sanded all voids and odd contours flush, taking care to preserve as much detail as possible—masking tape protected adjacent detail. I painted the interior of the engine cowlings zinc chromate and cemented the painted engines

Fig. 19

inside. Once completed, the wings and horizontal stabilizers were attached to the fuselage.

I detailed the main landing gear struts by adding a brass brake cylinder and solder hydraulic lines (Fig. 14). I enhanced the tread pattern with a slotting file, then flattened the bottom of the tire to give the model a realistic sit.

Gun turrets. B-17Fs featured several different upper turret styles, none of which exactly matched the one in the Monogram kit. I slightly modified the kit turret by first sanding off all the framing detail. Next, I carved small recesses at the base for the retaining bolts. I filed the elevation slots a bit wider and installed shields that I turned from acrylic rod (Fig. 15). The finished turret was installed after the model was painted (Fig. 16).

The ball turret could have been used as is but I wanted to simulate the hemispherical fairings that were sometimes fitted to the sides of the turret and covered the supports. I spliced .030" styrene between the halves to make the turret perfectly round, then opened the sides (Fig. 17). The clear hemispherical fairings were turned in the lathe from acrylic rod stock. To simulate the fairing's wire framework and other support details visible inside, I scored the inside of the acrylic, filled the scored lines with neutral gray paint (Fig. 18), backed the paint with gap-filling super glue, rechucked them in the lathe, and sanded down the excess glue.

I milled cutouts for the turret support arms and cemented the gun assembly in place with a few additional details followed by the end caps. I cut the ends off the supports so they fit into the cutouts in the fairing. I'm happy with

the three-dimensional look achieved in the finished turret (Fig. 19).

Paint and decals. I masked off all the openings and clear portions (Fig. 20). I used a medium tack frisket for all the windows while the astrocompass, nose cone, and turrets were protected with a combination of tape and a liquid mask.

I mixed all the colors from Floquil lacquers which stand up well to various weathering techniques applied over them. The variations in World War Two

aircraft finishes are endless, so I used Federal Standard 595a color chips only as a rough guide to establish olive drab, neutral gray, and medium green. I wanted to model a relatively new replacement aircraft serving with the 91st Bomb Group in the spring of 1943, so I chose fresh paint colors.

The underside of the aircraft was neutral gray and the topside olive drab. Before I applied the underside gray, I sprayed around the windows with the olive drab to prevent gray overspray from

Fig. 20

Fig. 21

Fig. 22

showing through the windows. The entire underside was then sprayed gray. After allowing it to dry for a day, I rubbed the entire model with a 3M gray Scuff Pad which produces a smooth finish.

I masked the gray areas with 3M Fineline tape and masking tape. Fineline tape has sharper edges than regular masking tape, but I still cut a fresh edge for a sharp color demarcation line. 3M Scuff Pads and Fineline tape are available at auto paint stores. Then I applied olive drab to the entire aircraft. To simulate the slightly raised framework around the enlarged cheek windows, I masked around the frames and airbrushed a couple more coats of olive drab.

By tinting the basic olive drab paint, I accented random panels. Fabric-covered control surfaces faded faster than metal surfaces, so I sprayed them with a lighter olive

drab tint. Many early B-17s had center fin sections manufactured and painted by a subcontractor. Sometimes they were painted medium green, so I used Floquil Pullman Green (No. 110045).

I then removed all masking and rubbed down the olive drab with the scuff pad. I protected the control surfaces since I wanted to retain their slightly textured finish. The deicer boots were masked and painted flat black. Next, I lightly weathered with different shades of olive drab and black to simulate fading and exhaust stains, then I lightly scribed the outline of the window frames into the paint.

The decals for my "Wabash Cannonball" came from Microscale (now Super Scale) sheet No. 48-21, and insignias came from various sheets in my spares box. The documentation on this aircraft is inconsistent, but I used a picture

in Squadron/Signal Publications' original B-17 in action as my reference. Decals were carefully trimmed and applied using liberal amounts of Microset and Solvaset. Using the scuffing pad left a semigloss finish, so I didn't need clear gloss underneath the decals to prevent silvering.

After letting the decals dry for a few days, I airbrushed the entire model with Testor's Dullcote. Duplicating the practice of the day, I oversprayed the insignias with light gray to reduce the contrast and improve the camouflage. A little more weathering with the airbrush, washes, and dry-brushing followed (Figs. 21 and 22).

The final touches were the guns and gun barrels, tail gun sight, and antennas, which I made from brass wire and fishing line. My model of the classic B-17F is complete.

DETAILING AN A-10A TANK KILLER FROM MASSACHUSETTS

Improving Tamiya's 1/48 scale kit

Brett added many details not found in the MRC-Tamiya A-10A kit, including an updated ejection seat. In addition to the techniques explained in the text, Brett split and opened the wing-tip speed brakes.

ESCI's 1/48 scale ground support set provided the ordnance loading truck and the ground crew.

BY BRETT VECHIARELLI

The Fairchild Republic A-l0A Thunderbolt II may not be beautiful, but to friendly troops and armor drivers it's a welcome sight. Armed with a 30 mm Avenger cannon, freefall bombs, and Maverick missiles, a pair of "Warthogs" maneuvering at treetop level can lay armament on a target every eight seconds!

The A-10 I chose to model was from the 104th Tactical Fighter Group of the Massachusetts Air National Guard. Since I live only ten miles away from the unit's home base, I arranged a tour and took detailed photos of the actual aircraft to help detail my model.

Building the heads-up display (HUD). I scratch-built the heads-up display frame, Fig. 1, by first drawing it on tracing paper with a drafting pencil and a small straightedge. Next came the tedious process of building both sides of the frame from .010" Plastruct plastic rod (No MR-10). Make two sides,

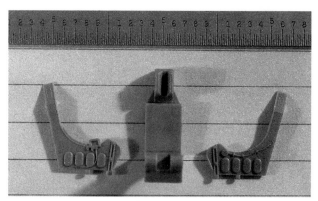

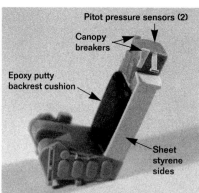

Fig. 2. A-10A Head up display frame pattern

Fig. 1, left. The author's scratchbuilt head-up display is clearly visible behind the kit windscreen.

Fig. 3. MRC-Tamiya's kit comes with the original ESCAPAC ejection seat.

following the template in Fig. 2. I used thin stretched sprue to apply small amounts of super glue to each frame joint. Glue the outside edges first, then measure, cut, and fit the inside segments. After the frame dries thoroughly, separate it from the paper template by shaving it off with a razor blade. Attach the two frames to the instrument panel coaming with liquid cement, then airbrush them flat black. Finally, add clear acetate to represent the HUD glass.

Revamping the ejection seat. MRC-Tamiya's kit comes with the ESCAPAC IE-9 ejection seat used in early A-10s and F-15s. These aircraft now carry the ACES II seat, so I converted the kit seat to the new standard. The seat comes in three parts—the main body and the left and right sides, Fig. 3. First, shave off most of the headrest and file the top quarter flush with the main structure. Attach the sides, cementing only along the seat cushion. When the glue has set, remove the top of the sides, Fig. 4. Next, box in the lower part of the headrest with strip styrene.

Form a backrest cushion from epoxy putty, Fig. 5. Build up the sides with strips of .020" sheet styrene. Attach small pieces of strip styrene to the top of the seat to represent the canopy breakers and carve two pitot-pressure sensors from stretched sprue. I used Waldron's seat belt set for the lap belts and shoulder harnesses, Fig. 6, and made the emergency oxygen bottle on the left side of the seat from stretched sprue and fine wire. Install launch rails made from Plastruct channel stock, then paint the seat gray with khaki belts and cushions.

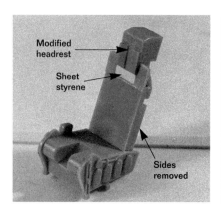

Fig. 4. The first step in seat conversion is removing the sides and modifying the headrest.

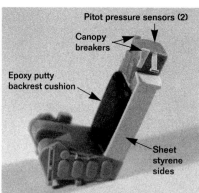

Fig. 5. The converted seat is beginning to look like the ACES II.

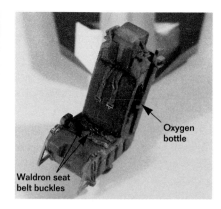

Fig. 6. Brett's finished ACES II seat includes realistic seat belt buckles.

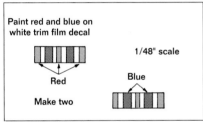

Paint red and blue on
white trim film decal

1/48" scale

Red

Blue

Make two

**Fig. 7. Air Force Outstanding Unit
Award ribbon**

Red decal stripes

White stars

Black Massachusetts outline

MA
620

**Fig. 8, top. The Outstanding Unit Award ribbons were made by painting red
and blue on white decal trim film, then positioned on the fuselage sides.**

**Fig. 9. The markings of the Massachusetts Air Guard were produced by cut-
ting stripes from red decal trim film. The stars were cut from Microscale
sheet No. 48-135.**

Special markings. Microscale (now Super Scale International) sheet No. 48-135 includes the basic Massachusetts Air Guard decals, but I made the following additional updated markings: an Outstanding Unit Award ribbon on both sides of the fuselage, twin red stripes with white stars on the top of each tail, and a black Massachusetts state symbol with a green

"104th" on the right engine pod.

All my custom decals were made by airbrushing Tamiya acrylic paints onto clear or colored Super Scale International trim film 6" x 9" solid-color, water-slide decal sheets found in well stocked hobby shops. I used vernier calipers, a small straightedge, and a draftsman's pencil to map out the width of the red and blue

stripes of the Outstanding Unit Award on a sheet of white trim film (TF-01), Fig. 7. I masked everything but the two thick blue sections with small pieces of masking tape cut to size with a razor blade, then sprayed blue. After the blue areas were dry, I masked over them, removed the strips for the red sections, and sprayed red paint. The painted area

Fig. 10. Dry-transfer numbers and letters were applied to clear decal film. The Massachusetts state outline was used as a mask for flat black paint.

was cut in half to form the two ribbons, Fig. 8.

The red tail stripes wrap around the outside of the top of the tails to the inside surfaces of each rudder. These can be made from red trim film or by airbrushing red paint on clear decal film. The clusters of five white stars were made by removing stars from the Microscale sheet and placing them in position on the red stripes, Fig. 11.

The outline of the state of Massachusetts was a little more tricky. First I applied dry-transfer numbers and letters (104th) to clear decal sheet. Next I reduced the outline of the state from an encyclopedia illustration with a reducing copy machine. I cut away along the outline and used the sheet as a stencil, Fig. 10. After attaching the stencil to the clear decal sheet, I sprayed on flat black paint. When the paint was dry I carefully removed the numbers and letters with tape, revealing unpainted clear decal film below. When the decal is placed on the model, the model's green paint shows through the clear numbers and letters.

And that's not all! The MRC-Tamiya kit is a good one, but I made more changes. Rather than go into detail, I'll just point out some of my modifications: Air brakes were opened and hydraulic and electrical lines were inserted using wire; the accelerometer standby compass and gun camera switch were added to the cockpit; left and right engine and APU fire pull handles were added to the instrument panel; rear view mirrors were installed on the canopy bow; the gun barrels and muzzle vents were drilled out; brake lines on the landing gear struts were simulated with fine wire; and I added sway braces to the weapons pylons.

Posing the model on a realistic base creates a miniature scene of typical air base action. I used crew figures and equipment from ESCI's Aircraft Support Group (kit No. 4025) for the finishing touch. It was fun adding details to an already excellent kit. Just a little extra work can make your model unique.

REFERENCES

• Bell, Dana *A-10 Warthog in Detail & Scale*, Kalmbach Publishing Co., Waukesha, Wisconsin, 1993
• Bell, Dana, *Colors & Markings of the A-10 Warthog*, Kalmbach Publishing Co., Waukesha, Wisconsin, 1994.
• Drendel, Lou, *A-10 Warthog in Action*, Squadron/Signal Publications, Carrollton, Texas, 1981
• Spick, Mike, *Modern Combat Aircraft 28, A-10 Thunderbolt II*, Ian Allan Ltd., London, 1987
• Sweetman, Bill, *Modern Fighting Aircraft, A-10 Thunderbolt II*, Arco Publishing Inc., New York, 1985
• *USAF A-10A Flight Manual*

SOURCES

• Sheet styrene: Evergreen Scale Models, 12808 N. E. 125th Way, Kirkland, WA 98034
• Plastic rod and channel: Plastruct, 1020 S. Wallace Pl., City of Industry, CA 91748
• Decal trim film: Super Scale International, 2211 Mouton Dr., Carson City, NV 89706
• Photoetched detail parts: Waldron Model Products, P. O. Box 431, Merlin, OR 97532

DETAILING AND DAMAGING A 1/32 SCALE FW 190F-8

Realistic battle damage and weathering techniques

Fig. 1. Parked in fresh snow after a combat mission over the Eastern Front, this Fw 190F-8 displays significant flak damage. Actually, it's author Greg Hildebrandt's 1/32 scale model parked in baking soda. The backdrop is the edge of a woodland and the lighting is sun and sky. Note the absence of the lower part of the main landing gear covers.

Fig. 2. This close-up shows the flak damage. The realistic torn metal is torn aluminum foil. Note the small bullet holes forward of the large hole in the fuselage.

BY GREG HILDEBRANDT

A realistic model is the goal of all modelers, and wear and tear help produce that effect. Combat aircraft go through more weathering (wear) I and damage (tear) than any other aircraft. Realistically producing these ill effects isn't as difficult as it may seem.

The inspiration for my model was Squadron/Signal Publications' book Focke Wulf FW 190 in Action (1975). This first volume on the classic Luftwaffe fighter included pictures of an Fw 190A-4 that landed safely after being struck by Soviet flak over the Eastern Front. Although not the same aircraft, I fell in love with

the back cover illustration of a Hungary-based Fw 190F-8 in winter camouflage in January 1945. I decided to model that aircraft and incorporate the battle damage of the Fw 190A-4.

I chose the 1/32 scale Hasegawa Focke Wulf Fw 190 for this project because it offers optional parts for the 190Fs, including the

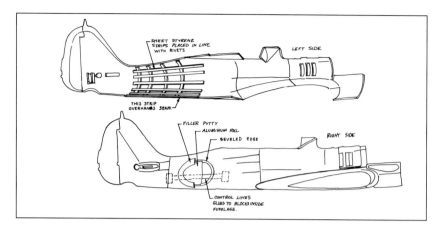

Fig. 3. Fuselage details

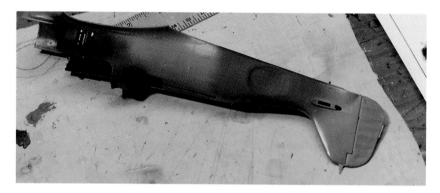

Fig. 4. The flak-damaged area is covered with aluminum foil faired into the fuselage with filler putty. Note that the area is slightly concave.

bulged cover for the cowling guns, wing cannons, bombs, and drop tank. To retain the sleek look of the fighter, I left off the center line and wing bomb racks; in service, these were sometimes removed.

Destruction construction. Rather than superdetail the engine and interior, I decided to spend time on the exterior, simulating battle damage. I normally use super glue to assemble my models—I find it faster and stronger than solvent cements. If parts are carefully prefitted and don't require extensive positioning, super glue works well.

Most construction was out of the box—this is a good kit and I made no major changes. Before joining the fuselage halves, start the battle damage to the right rear

fuselage half. Drill holes around the perimeter of the damaged area, then use a knife to cut from one hole to the next to remove the plastic. Make the hole larger than intended—you'll see why later. Detail the interior of the left fuselage section with styrene strip frame members, Fig. 3. The bottom strip also hides the fuselage seam.

The two control lines that survived the blast and enabled the pilot to return home are mounted inside the right side section. I made these from fine music wire, in this case dulcimer strings. They are mounted to blocks of styrene on each side of the hole. Squares of styrene with a score for the wire to fit into are glued on top to secure them. Before closing the

fuselage, apply a coat of medium gray to the inside.

Use heavy-duty aluminum foil to simulate the damaged sheet metal on the fuselage. When done properly, it's excellent for simulating tears and wrinkles. Cut the foil to shape with about a 3/32" overlap around the hole. Before attaching it, bevel the edges of the hole with a grinding bit on a motor tool so the foil can be positioned slightly below the surface. Glue the foil in place with super glue, but first sand the inside edge of the foil to ensure good adhesion. The foil section will be flat in the center, and that's okay. It will be opened in the center, and the edges will look slightly caved in from the flak blast, Fig. 4.

After the super glue has set, carefully fill around the edges with filler putty. Use small amounts and do a neat job to avoid excessive sanding near the foil. Take care not to get filler on the center where the hole will be. Sand, prime, and inspect the filled area before continuing.

Tubular detailing. Some of the details I added were made with aluminum and brass tubing, available at most hardware and hobby stores. Fashion the side exhaust stacks from 1/8" (outside diameter) aluminum tubing, slightly flattened to the proper cross section. After sanding, mount them to the inside of the engine cowling. Carefully test fit to be sure the engine cowling will fit over the engine and the new stacks.

Use 3/32" aluminum tubing for the four belly exhaust pipes (don't flatten these). Install them in an angled slot made by drilling several holes with a drill bit. Finish the tubes with sandpaper and install them with super glue, Fig. 5.

Fig. 5. Greg replaced the molded-in exhaust stacks of the kit with small-diameter aluminum tubing.

Make the four wing gun barrels with 1/16" brass tubing and install them before closing the wing halves. The inboard barrels pass through the wheel wells, so drill holes for them, Fig. 6. Open holes in the leading edge of the wing halves with a knife and round file—these holes are slightly larger than the gun barrels. Cut the gun barrels by rolling them back and forth underneath a sharp knife.

To align the gun barrels, mount the back ends on styrene pads, which will be glued to the bottom wing halves. The elevation of the guns can be adjusted by sliding the pads back and forth. When you get it right, cement the pads to the wing and the barrels to the pads.

A few more details. Cement short sections of plastic or vinyl wire insulation over the muzzles of the nose guns. To give the aircraft a candid look, cut the elevator surfaces from the tail planes and reattach them angled down, Fig. 7. Reposition the control stick in the cockpit if you do this—down elevator, stick forward.

Painting. Before you paint, let me show you my method for masking around canopy frames. Use frosted cellophane tape and mask one section at a time. As it comes off the roll, the edges of the tape aren't sharp and sometimes collect dirt and dust, so apply the tape to a piece of glass and cut new edges with a sharp blade. The tape is applied along the frame edge and the other edges of the clear panel are cut as the tape rests on the canopy, Fig. 8. Compound curves must be covered by cutting expansion slits so the tape can conform or by using several pieces of tape.

Don't cut too deep through the tape, use a straightedge whenever possible, and trim curves slightly wide to the paint side to leave room for errors.

After painting the canopy, remove the canopy mask by lifting a corner of the tape with tweezers. Pull the tape slowly to prevent it from tearing. Some adhesive will be left behind, but it's easy to remove. Press fresh tape onto the residue and pull it up. Since the adhesive sticks better to itself than to plastic, the tape does the trick.

After masking the cockpit, wheel wells, and engine, paint the entire model with light gray primer. Check for defects, then paint the aircraft in the camouflage colors: pale duck-egg belly with

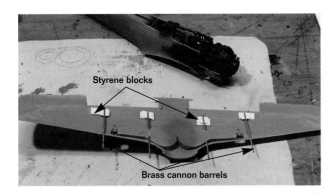

Fig. 6. The brass-tubing cannon barrels are adjusted with styrene blocks. Note how the inboard barrels pass through the main gear wheel wells.

Fig. 7. As an added touch, Greg cut the elevators from the horizontal stabilizers and reattached them in the "down" position.

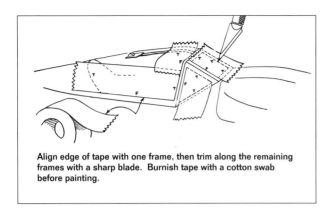

Align edge of tape with one frame, then trim along the remaining frames with a sharp blade. Burnish tape with a cotton swab before painting.

Fig. 8. Masking canopies

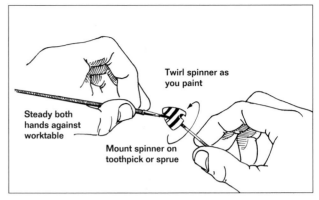

Twirl spinner as you paint

Steady both hands against worktable

Mount spinner on toothpick or sprue

Fig. 10. Painting spirals on spinners

Fig. 9. Realistic weathering helps make this model a winner. Brown paint splattered on with a toothbrush simulates mud around the landing gear.

medium and dark green upper surfaces. The fuselage sides receive the common speckled camouflage.

Before decaling, spray on a coat of clear gloss to improve decal adhesion. Painting the random winter white camouflage comes after decaling since the ground crews applied this in the field and sprayed it around the markings.

Easy ways to weather. Next comes detailing and weathering with paint. Spray a brownish dark gray around the exhaust pipes and gun ports. When all paint is dry, accent the control surface hinge lines and access panels with India ink and a Rapidograph technical pen. I use No. 0 and 00 pens and a sheet styrene straightedge when the model doesn't feature recessed lines. The styrene straightedge can bend around the fuselage and be taped in place. Apply masking tape just under and behind the edge of the styrene to raise the edge off the model and prevent

ink from running underneath. The ink is permanent and will be sealed with the final flat clear coat.

Now you can weather the plane further using oil pastels such as Cray-pas. Simulate wear on access panels, walkways, and leading edges of the wing and tail planes with silver paint applied sparingly with a fine brush. Use masking tape occasionally to keep the "paint chips" on one side of a panel.

To simulate spattered mud, first airbrush mud brown streaks aligned with the wheels on the underside of the wing from front to rear, Fig. 9. For larger splatters, dip an old toothbrush into the paint and apply it by dragging a finger across the bristles. Practice this on an old model first. More paint on the brush produces larger droplets. Splatter both the main gear struts and around the tail wheel.

Here's how to paint those spirals on spinners. Mount the spinner on a toothpick or piece of sprue—this acts as a handle. Next, paint the spinner flat white. When the white is dry, paint black by steadying your hands against the worktable and twirling the spinner in one hand while holding the paintbrush in the other, Fig. 10. Stick the axle in a chunk of plastic foam or modeling clay to let the spinner dry.

Flak damage. Finish the battle damage after painting. First, open the flak blast hole in the fuselage by inserting a knife in the center of the foil-covered area. Open the hole by working your way out from the center with the knife and tweezers. Tear away pieces and pierce holes in the foil to simulate shrapnel damage. Next, spray a light coat of dark brownish gray paint. Lock the damaged foil in place with super glue and touch up the edges of the holes with silver paint. A final coat of clear flat will give a realistic finish.

If you also want to add bullet holes, heat a safety or straight pin over a gas flame until the metal glows

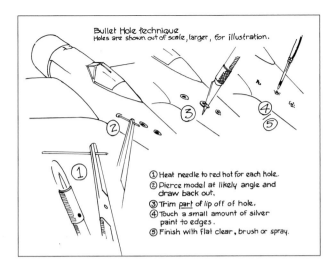

Bullet Hole technique
Holes are shown out of scale, larger, for illustration.

① Heat needle to red hot for each hole.
② Pierce model at likely angle and draw back out.
③ Trim part of lip off of hole.
④ Touch a small amount of silver paint to edges.
⑤ Finish with flat clear, brush or spray.

Fig. 11

deep red. Hold the pin with needle-nose pliers or a hemostat (a surgical clamping tool). Insert the pin through the plastic at an angle a bullet would likely take, then remove it quickly, Fig. 11. Reheat the pin for each hole.

Next, remove part of the raised lip around each bullet hole with a knife and touch silver paint around the edges to simulate chipped paint. A coat of clear flat tones down the silver to a believable sheen.

Final details. I used guitar strings for the small whip antenna and the pitot tube on the wing. Remove the outer winding to get the look of a shaft within a tube.

The wheel covers of Focke Wulfs were often removed to prevent snow and mud buildup on the main wheels. I cut off that portion of the kit covers. I wanted a little snow on the tires, so I coated them with super glue and rolled them through baking soda. The combination sets immediately and looks like icy snow. As a final touch, use a file and sandpaper to flatten the bottom of the tires so the model looks as though it has some weight to it. Glue the tires to the struts, rotating them until the flat area meets the ground. Fine tune this effect by holding each tire while moving sandpaper back and forth on the work surface underneath.

Snow scene photography. I photographed my finished winter scheme Fw 190F-8 against the most realistic winter backdrop I could find—real trees and real snow! First, I made the base from Masonite and covered it with baking soda "snow" applied with a sifter. Piling it up on the back edge of the scene helps blend into the real background. I made tracks in the snow by pushing the model through it several

times. Then I placed the base on a platform (you can use two chairs, a picnic table, or a pair of sawhorses) and the camera on a tripod. Elevating everything makes photography more comfortable and allows you to adjust the camera angle to produce the proper background perspective.

To produce photos that look like they were shot by a photographer standing next to the real airplane, determine "scale eye level." For 1/32 scale, position the center of the camera lens 2¼" above the base (six scale feet). This will create a realistic perspective with lots of sky and background. Avoid including foreground as it will probably be out of focus.

To achieve sufficient depth of field (objects both far away and close to the camera in focus), small apertures (f stops) are needed. The smallest aperture on most cameras is f16 or f22. Small apertures mean long shutter speeds to compensate for the reduced level of light striking the film. A tripod is essential to prevent camera movement during the long exposure.

Once you have set up, concentrate on composition and lighting angle. For most shots outdoors you'll want to use the most realistic light available—sun and sky. Pick a site such as an airport or meadow where the tree line is well back (a large tree trunk or the corner of your garage in the photo ruins the realism). Turn the model and move the camera until you find the best background, lighting angle, and subject perspective. Study the setting carefully and look for parts of the model that may be lost in the background. Adjust the angles until these clear up.

I used a Canon AT-1 with a 50 mm lens and 400 ISO black-and-white and color films for these shots.

SOURCES

• **Sheet styrene: Evergreen Scale Models, 12808 N. E. 125th Way, Kirkland, WA 98034**
• **Brass tubing: K&S Engineering, 6917 W. 59th St., Chicago, IL 80638**

MODELING WOOD FLIGHT DECKS

Simple bases that will set off your models

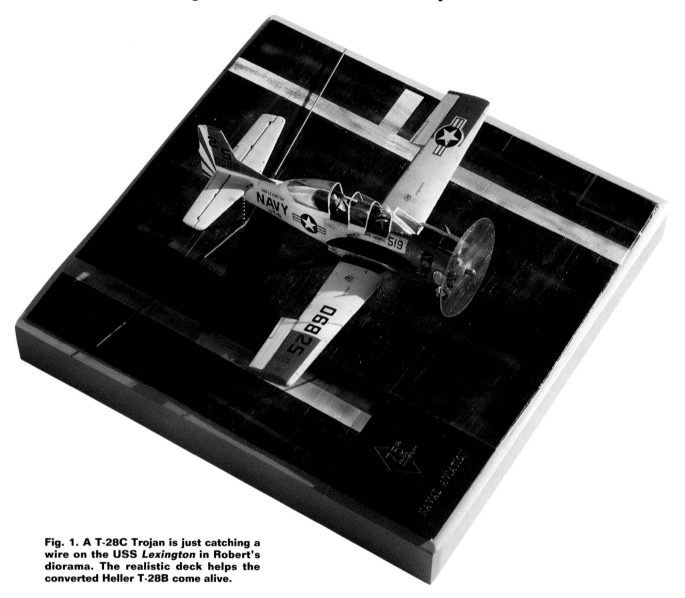

Fig. 1. A T-28C Trojan is just catching a wire on the USS *Lexington* in Robert's diorama. The realistic deck helps the converted Heller T-28B come alive.

BY ROBERT DOUGLAS O'DONOVAN

The best way to display a model is to place it in its natural setting, and what better place for a Navy airplane than on a carrier deck? At an IPMS regional convention some time back I had the pleasure of winning awards in the aircraft diorama category, and what surprised me most was that the questions I received were not about the aircraft but about the

carrier decks. I use a quick and inexpensive method to obtain an authentic deck for World War Two and prewar aircraft.

As with any project, good information is a must. Numerous plans and photos of wood-deck carriers are available. Although mine is a generic American deck, you can build one based on a specific ship using the same methods. Common coloring for U. S. flight decks was red-brown stain before WWII and

Fig. 2. Alternating strips of bass-wood and styrene are laid down to make the deck. Individual planks aren't yet scribed. The overhang will be trimmed after gluing.

purple-blue stain during the war. This contrasts with gray or black which is often seen in dioramas. Add to this the question of white or yellow deck markings and you have a real controversy. With good references, however, you can be confident of an excellent setting for display or photography.

A flight deck is made of wood planks separated at intervals by steel frames; pre-*Essex*-class carriers typically had seven planks between frames, but this number varied. Later ships had more planks between frames. In 1/72 scale, the planks will each be about 3/32" wide. The metal frames served several purposes, but mainly provided a place where aircraft were tied down. The U-shaped holes running the length of the frames are tie-down holes. These were necessary, as tie-down points in the wood planks would have been impractical. Later carriers with steel flight decks eliminated the need for frames, as tie-downs could be incorporated in the deck plates.

The deck is highlighted by the contrast between wooden planks and metal frames. I use basswood sheets to simulate Douglas fir planks and sheet styrene for the metal frames. Nothing I have tried simulates wood better than wood, no matter what finish is applied, and styrene simulates metal well.

Beginning construction. You need to make several decisions before beginning construction. Scale is

obviously the first choice. I build in 1/72 scale, but you could use 1/48 or 1/32 scale. The size will determine how much material is needed and whether you'll use a plain deck or one with an elevator. I had a 15" x 19" piece of plywood, large enough to hold several aircraft and include an elevator.

Wood and steel. Start with basswood sheets (available at model railroad shops) and a T-square. Cut the basswood to the proper width between frames, about 5/8" in 1/72 scale. Don't worry about individual plank size yet. Another method is to use pre-scribed sheets, although hiding a joint line if you butt ends together is difficult.

Evergreen Scale Models makes styrene strips .060" x .125" (No. 156-B), which are close to the proper scale size for the metal frames.

Laying it down. The length of the basswood sheets isn't critical as long as they overlap your base. If you're making a deck without an elevator. simply glue alternating strips of basswood and styrene strip, Fig. 2. Use a good contact cement such as Weldwood (available in hardware stores). I butt the edges even with one side of the base, overlapping the other side. Flip the base over and trim the overlap with a sharp knife. Using the T-square, mark 3/32" intervals on the wood sections. Then scribe individual planks with a sharp knife.

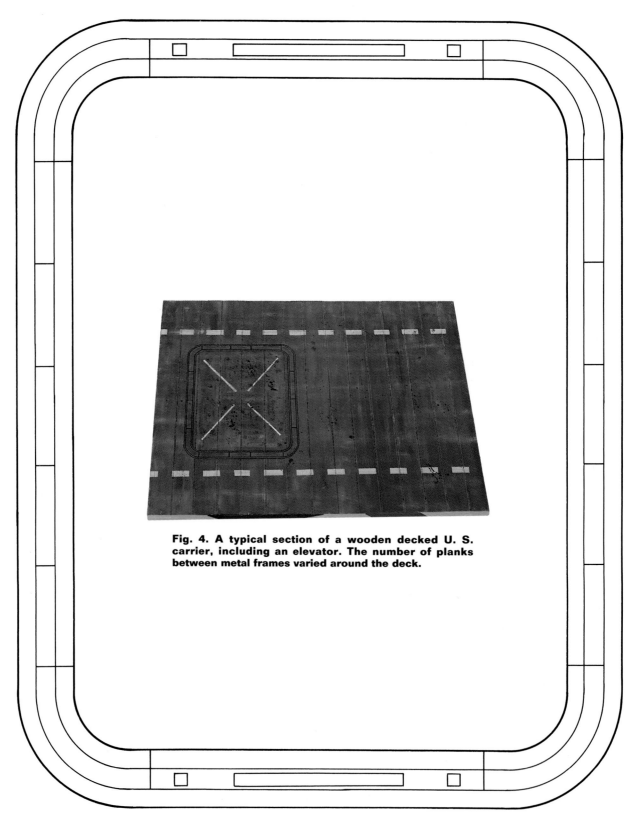

Fig. 4. A typical section of a wooden decked U. S. carrier, including an elevator. The number of planks between metal frames varied around the deck.

Fig. 3. Typical elevator   1/72 scale

Elevator. When including an elevator, I prepare full-size drawings of the metal elevator frame, Fig 3, and trace them onto a sheet of styrene. When cut out, the sheet gives me a template, as well as the elevator itself.

To incorporate the elevator, position the template before the planks are laid down, trace along the elevator, and measure its location from the corners. When you apply cement to the base, leave a clear area over the outline, and completely cover the base with planking and frames. Lay the template back down on the planking, using the measurements you took from the corners and trace around the edges. Cut out the planking under the elevator frame with a sharp knife. The elevator template can then be inserted and painted as part of the completed elevator.

Tie-downs. To reproduce the tie-downs I make decals. Other than clear decal paper, you'll need access to a copy machine that can enlarge and reduce, or use a commercial outlet. Draw the tie-downs large, which is easier to work with, then reduce them to the scale you need, Fig. 5. To draw the U-shaped tie-downs, use an architect's template (available at art supply stores).

I make several strips of tie-downs in a large size, copy them, and tape the copies to the original to give me a full sheet of large tie-downs ready for reduction. In 1/72 scale the tie-down should fit on a strip 3/32" wide. Experiment to find the amount of reduction to use.

Making your own decals. Next we'll turn these drawings into decals. Tape the corners of a sheet of clear decal to copy machine paper. Insert this into the paper tray, clear side up. Place the properly reduced drawing on the copy plate of the machine and hit the print button. You should get a decal sheet of tie-downs; cut them out and apply as you would commercial decals.

Painting. For deck stain, I use Polly S mixed to a purple-blue. An exact match will be difficult even if you have a paint chip or color photograph. For prewar, a reddish brown mixed with flat white works well. I add black and silver to the mix for the frames and elevator. Use a gloss before applying the tie-down decals. I also use decals for the yellow stripes as decals are easier than masking and painting deck lines. A final coat of flat finish seals them in place.

Add weathering using your favorite methods. I take the base color add flat white, and dry-brush. Black diluted three-to-one with water can be run across the planks for added highlights. Finally, I brush on pastel chalk powder to simulate sun and salt water bleaching. You can add oil stains, but keep them to a minimum.

Completion. The last step is to add a sheet styrene edge around your base as a border for the deck. I paint this light gray for prewar or whatever color is correct for the period of your model.

When I landed on her, the *Lexington* (AVT-16) didn't have tie-down frames. Paint her deck dark blue-gray with a neutral gray edge. The *Lexington* is heavily used, so don't be bashful with weathering. There you have it, a quick and inexpensive diorama setting. I was able to build two decks for under $20.00.

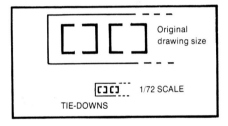

Fig. 5

SOURCES

• **Styrene strips: Evergreen Scale Models, 12808 N. E. 125th Way, Kirkland, WA 98034**
• **Paint: Floquil Polly S, Route 30 North, Amsterdam, NY 12010-9204**

DETAILING A 1/48 SCALE KOREAN WAR CORSAIR

Improving Hasegawa's F4U-4

Fig. 1. The F4U-4 was the most common Corsair version of the Korean War. Alain made his model from the 1/48 scale Hasegawa kit with colorful markings from Super Scale International.

BY ALAIN PELLETIER

I've always been fascinated by Vought's "bent-wing bird" and I always wanted to build a good Korean War Corsair for my 1/48 scale collection. The Hasegawa F4U-4 Corsair is the best kit of this version, with accurate outlines and crisp detail. Although I considered building it right out of the box, I decided to incorporate as many improvements as I could.

Cockpit. I tried to duplicate the cockpit details in the color drawings on page 17 of Squadron/Signal's *F4U Corsair in Color*.

Using sheet styrene and stretched sprue, add detail to the cockpit tub (part No. A6) and the rear bulkhead (B5). I decided to scratch-build the seat from sheet styrene (Figs. 4 and 5), then added foil harnesses with photoetched buckles from Model Technologies set No. MT0005.

To simulate the visible fuselage structure, use Evergreen styrene strips (Fig. 6). On the right side, add an oxygen regulator and hose, and on the left side, the throttle, engine controls, trimtab wheel, pump handle, and wing folding actuator handle. Paint the

cockpit Interior Green (Humbrol 158) and dry-brush with aluminum to simulate wear. Paint the instrument panel matte black and dry-brush with flat white, then add tiny drops of clear gloss on each instrument face. The final touches to the instrument panel are the weapons switch boxes and the gunsight on top.

Engine and cowling. Unfortunately, Hasegawa molded only the front half of the front row of cylinders of the R2800-18W engine. You could substitute an engine from a Monogram P-61, but I tried to make the best of the kit engine.

Fig. 2. Alain dropped the flaps on his model, accenting the Corsair's bent-wing appearance.

Fig. 3. Alain also added cockpit details, opened the starboard gun bay, and opened the cowl flaps to show off his scratchbuilt engine mount.

Fig. 4

Fig. 5

Fig. 6

First, paint the bulkhead (molded with the cylinders) black, the cylinders aluminum, the crankcase and oil sump medium gray, and the bolts and push-rods silver.

I had an opportunity to examine a real Corsair at an air show. When the aircraft isn't flying, it usually has its cowl flaps open, revealing lots of detail around the engine mount. I just had to show this on my model even though the modifications to the kit would be time-consuming.

To make the back of your engine appear more realistic, first cut out the cowl flaps from the fuselage halves with a razor saw and cut off all the exhaust pipes. Add a bulkhead from sheet styrene, then fashion the engine mount from Evergreen styrene rod (Fig. 7). I made mine after studying a Corsair maintenance manual (Fig. 8).

Paint the mount interior green, then fashion

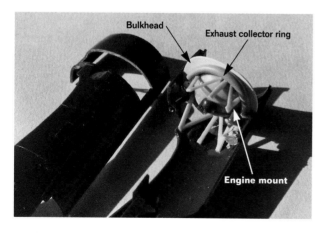

Bulkhead

Exhaust collector ring

Engine mount

Fig. 7

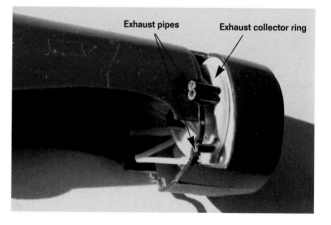

Exhaust pipes

Exhaust collector ring

Fig. 9

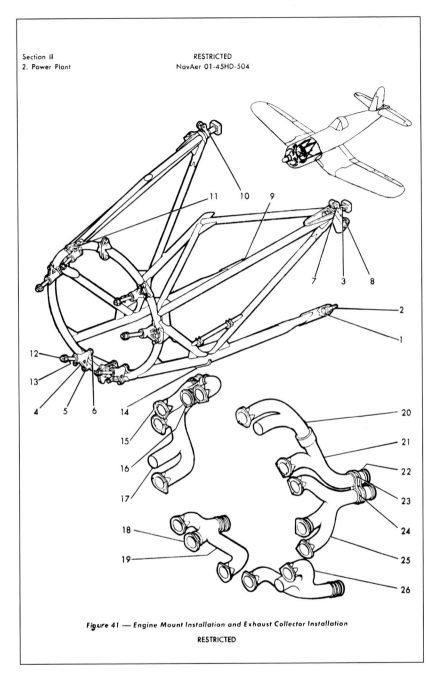

Figure 41 — Engine Mount Installation and Exhaust Collector Installation

RESTRICTED

Fig. 8

Fig. 10

the exhaust collector ring from 4mm-diameter plastic rod heated and shaped to fit onto the bulkhead. Add six short pieces of plastic tube for the exhaust pipes, then paint these and the ring gunmetal (Fig. 9).

Cut new cowl flaps from .010" sheet styrene, curl them a little, mount them open, and support them with tiny stretched-sprue push rods (Fig. 10).

Wings. To drop the flaps on the Corsair, separate them from the upper and lower surfaces of the wing with a razor saw. Next, thin the trailing edge of the upper surface of the wing at the cut line; you won't need to thin the edge of the lower surface because it will be hidden by the lowered flaps. Assemble the flap parts and cement square styrene strip leading edges to each flap. Round off the leading edges with files and sandpaper (Fig. 11).

Before assembling the wing halves, drill out the three identification lights in the bottom of the right wing. Cut sections from stretched clear sprue and insert them in the holes (Fig. 12). Paint the inside faces of the clear plastic with silver, then mask the outside faces. After you paint the model, coat the lights with Tamiya or Gunze Sangyo clear red (forward), clear amber (middle), and clear green (aft).

Assemble the wing parts now, and don't forget the oil cooler and intercooler parts (Nos. E18 and E19). Improve the wing tip navigation lights by removing the scribed lights and replacing them with pieces of clear red (left) and green (right) toothbrush handle. File, sand, and polish them to shape.

You can improve the landing gear struts by adding retractor springs to the main gear (I used springs from the discontinued Verlinden coil spring set No. VP 045), and stretched-sprue brake lines.

Armament. Since the Corsair was used mainly in the ground attack role in Korea, I emphasized the

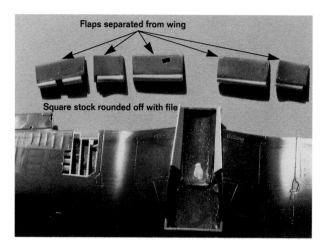

Fig. 11

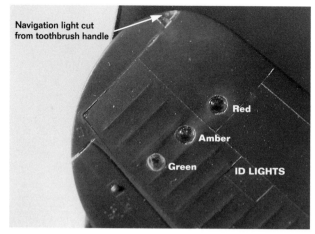

Fig. 12

armament on my model. To open the machine gun bay, cut the bay doors away with a razor saw and build the structure with thin sheet styrene (Fig. 13). Paint the bay Interior Green and lightly dry brush with flat aluminum paint.

I scratchbuilt the three .50-cal. machine guns, but you can substitute Verlinden's 1/48 scale P-51 Mustang detail set (No. VP 478). I used hand-corrugated strips of lead for the ammo belts and copper wire for the fire command wiring (Fig. 14). Cut new bay doors from .010" sheet styrene and pose them open after the model is painted.

Now you can install the flaps dropped. Add plastic rod flap actuators in the corners of the leading edges and thin sheet styrene triangles between the inboard and middle flaps.

To accent the ground attack role, substitute two 500 pound bombs (from Arii's F6F Hellcat) for the drop tanks in the Corsair kit. Thin the fins and add a stretched-sprue fuse to the front of each bomb.

Detail the bomb racks with stretched sprue. I made my bomb trolley from sheet styrene, Evergreen styrene strips, and the wheels from a Matchbox 1/76 scale armored car (Fig. 15).

The underwing "Zero-length" rocket launchers are the final detail. There are five launchers on

Fig. 13

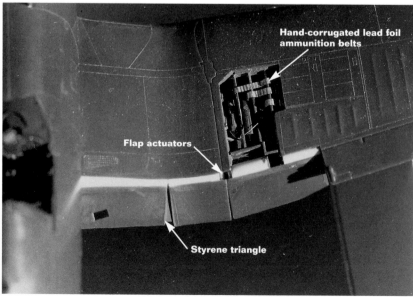

Fig. 14

Fig. 15

Fig. 16

each wing with two stubs each (Fig. 16). You can make them from sheet styrene.

Paint and decals. Corsairs were painted overall FS 15042 Glossy Sea Blue during the Korean War period. I wasn't happy with Humbrol's version of this color, so instead I chose Humbrol's Night Blue (HD3, discontinued). When you paint your model, make sure you mask the front and back of the cowl, the cockpit, the wheel and gun bays, and the lights.

Paint the landing gear struts flat aluminum with black brake lines and flat dark gray tires. Paint prop blades flat black with glossy yellow tips and Glossy Sea Blue hub. Paint three yellow bands on the nose of the olive drab bombs.

Personal and squadron markings on Navy and Marine aircraft were virtually absent during World War II, but they multiplied in the Korean War era. One of the most striking Corsair markings belonged to the F4U-4s of VMF323, a Marine squadron aboard the USS Sicily during the Inchon landings in September 1950.

I used Super Scale International sheet No.48-289, which features the rattlesnake-festooned Corsair. I had some trouble making the underwing "Marines" fit over the front outboard rocket launcher stub, so you may want to leave this stub off until you decal. A final coat of clear gloss seals the decals. Apply exhaust stains with an airbrush. I posed my Corsair on Verlinden's printed paper WWII carrier flight deck section.

I really enjoyed my Korean War Corsair project. I spent about 40 hours building and detailing it. It's a lot more colorful than the usual dull WWII Corsairs.

ACCURIZING TAMIYA'S 1/35 SCALE PANTHER AUSF A

World War Two German armor for the Eastern Front

Fig. 1. A scratchbuilt turret is the key element in a conversion that improves the accuracy of Tamiya's 1/35 scale Panther Ausf A kit. Tony Greenland's technique for modeling Zimmerit on armored vehicles enhances the realism of this German World War Two tank.

BY TONY GREENLAND
Artwork by the Author

British and Americans like to take credit for winning World War Two. In fact, the main land battles in the European theatre were fought on the Eastern Front against the Soviet Union, which ultimately defeated the majority of the German army. Consequently, German armaments in WWII were chiefly designed to combat Soviet tactics and weapons.

The tank in this chapter is an example of that strategy. The Panther Ausf A was conceived to combat the superb Soviet T34 tank. Zimmerit, a non-metallic paste applied to the exterior of German

tanks, was a defense against assaults by gallant Soviet infantry armed with magnetic mines.

The basic kit. The Panther Ausf A is an important vehicle to modelers of German WWII armor. In my opinion, Tamiya's version is its worst tank kit; the turret and mantlet are especially inaccurate. Yet there are few alternatives. Nichimo's Ausf G also suffers from scale inaccuracies, and to buy Gunze Sangyo's kit just to use the turret, road wheels, and tracks is too costly. So a conversion of the Tamiya kit is the path I chose.

Zimmerit. Zimmerit was applied by the manufacturers to all German tanks and assault guns between early 1943 and autumn 1944. Most of the Panther Ausf A tanks would have received this treatment. Later in the war, as Germany's tactics changed from offensive to defensive, the antimagnetic coating became unnecessary.

Zimmerit in miniature can be a nightmare for modelers. I use two techniques, although I prefer the method described below for most of my armored vehicles. For vehicles with a lot of broad surface area or little cast-on detail, I use Milliput epoxy putty; for smaller tanks (Panzer IV and smaller) I use a hot knife. Often I combine the two techniques.

Supplies. Some years ago my wife gave me the perfect tool for detailing Zimmerit. It's part of a shoe repair kit (for mending rubber soles) available from Woolworth's for about $1.50. The kit includes a metal scraper with two serrated edges, measuring 1¾" x ⅝". While many serrated alternatives exist, the size is perfect for handling and the grooves are in scale for 1/35. You'll also need an

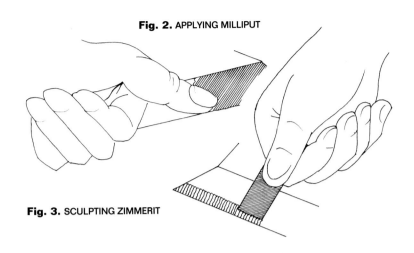

Fig. 2. APPLYING MILLIPUT

Fig. 3. SCULPTING ZIMMERIT

artist's plastic spatula and standard gray Milliput.

Preparation. Rough the surface of the plastic lightly to improve the adhesion of the Milliput. Some larger tank kits already have a rough cast to the plastic, which means you can skip this step. Work on only one or two surfaces per day. Until you master the technique mask any nearby surfaces which will not be covered.

Mix sufficient putty to cover the area selected. With a hard, pressing action, draw the Milliput toward you, Fig. 2. This should cover the working area with a coat of Milliput about 1 mm thick. Next, dip the spatula in water and use it to level and smooth the Milliput. The surface is now ready for modeling the Zimmerit texture.

Pattern details. The Zimmerit on Panthers was ridged vertically, then scored with a pattern of squares. Most other German armored vehicles had a horizontal pattern of ridges, and usually a Sturmgeschütz (assault gun) had a waffle pattern. Although it's not relevant to the Panther (because of the vertical pattern), the serrations of the ridging tool must be pointing down when used on other

vehicles. This is important to painting highlights, because a dark wash will lie in the recesses between the ridges.

Dip your finger in water and liberally spread the water over the area to be treated. Again starting furthest away from you, commence ridging, complete one row, Fig. 3, clean the tool, apply more water to the surface, and repeat. When one area is complete, remove the mask and clean up.

Allow the Milliput to dry for an hour. Then, using a set square (a draftsman's square or a T square) for a guide, use a knife to score the square pattern over the vertical ridges. Be careful not to flatten the ridges.

Other exterior details. Additional details require additional techniques. For large areas, position the detail part before applying the Zimmerit, outline it in pencil and mask the spot. Cut exactly around the shape and remove the surplus tape. After applying Zimmerit, remove the tape with a pin or knife while the Milliput is still wet. For small detail, press the object into the wet Milliput. Either carefully remove the Milliput with a fine knife and glue the part in place, or

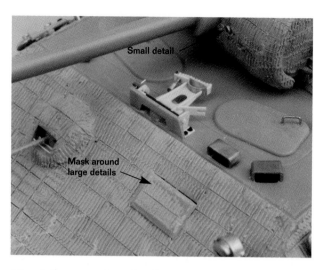

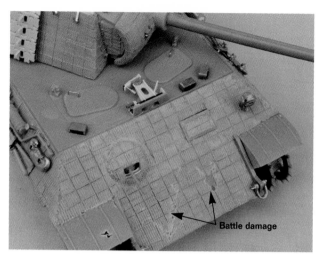

Fig. 4. Large surface details require careful masking to mark the boundaries of the Zimmerit around the object to be installed. Smaller details are easier—simply press them in place.

Fig. 5. Zimmerit is a good medium for modeling battle damage—it looks realistic and, because of its depth, it's in scale.

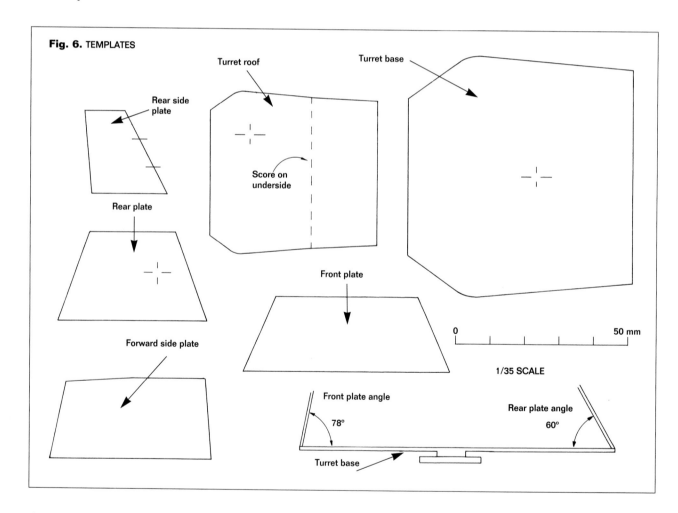

Fig. 6. TEMPLATES

Rear side plate

Turret roof

Turret base

Score on underside

Rear plate

Front plate

0   50 mm

1/35 SCALE

Forward side plate

Front plate angle
78°

Rear plate angle
60°

Turret base

just leave the object stuck in the Milliput, Fig. 4. Battle damage on Zimmerit surfaces looks more realistic and in scale because the Milliput will be approximately 0.5 mm thick, Fig. 5.

Scratchbuilding. A lot of modelers think scratchbuilding is highly advanced, but to me it is a natural

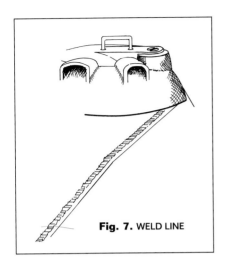

Fig. 7. WELD LINE

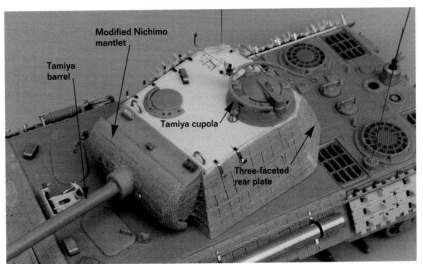

Fig. 8

Modified Nichimo mantlet

Tamiya barrel

Tamiya cupola

Three-faceted rear plate

Fig. 8, above right. Here is the completed turret. The Zimmerit coating serves double-duty here; it adds realism, and it hides conversions and modifications.

Figs. 9 and 9a, right. Tony's most complicated piece of superdetailing was this gun mount and traveling gunlock. (Inset) A closer look at the gun mount and lock.

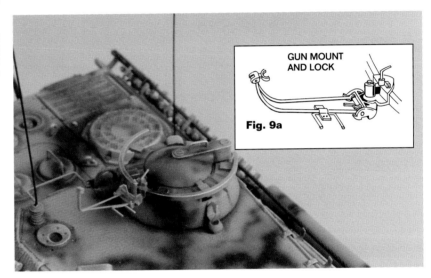

GUN MOUNT AND LOCK

Fig. 9a

Fig. 9

evolution from building kits straight from the box. These days I rarely buy kits, but I still manage to spend just as much—mostly on tools! Among the tools I consider indispensable are a variable-speed minidrill, soldering equipment, Historex Agents' punch and die set, Grandt Line nuts and bolts, and super glue.

Raw materials are equally important. Obviously, the main one is plastic, in sheets, strips, and rods. I often use brass, both in sheets of varying thicknesses (called shims, available from auto repair shops), and also exquisite, miniature structural shapes. In Europe I know of only one supplier, John Flack, and he sells solely by mail order. I like the fineness and strength of this material. On this model there was no requirement for special shapes. I used only brass wire, strip, and tubes.

Parts for the turret. The templates, Fig. 6, represent the full external measurements of the turret parts. To join other faces, the pieces should have a 45-degree beveled edge. For butt joints, deduct the plastic's thickness from the template. Other than the side walls of the turret, which should be two .020" sheets laminated together, the thickness of plastic is not important. I use .020" or .030" sheet. Since the turret will be covered with Zimmerit, the plastic's finish is not important.

The base is the starting point. Cut a hole in the sheet the same

Verlinden wire mesh

Fig. 10. The engine louvers are covered with Verlinden wire mesh.

diameter as Tamiya's base. This will allow access for reinforcement of the inner turret walls.

Next, cut the front plate, which should be glued to the base at the angle shown in Fig. 6. Repeat this step with the rear plate. Having assured yourself that the angles are correct and the lines are parallel, liberally apply super glue on the inside turret joints, then sprinkle baking powder on the super glue. This is an instant reinforcement to the joint that will enable subsequent work to be undertaken immediately.

Now cut out the roof (this should have butt joints). Score a line on the underside so you can bend the turret roof. Test fit the roof to the front and rear plates, once again confirming that angles and joints are perfect. After applying slow-setting plastic solvent

glue, check the fit, and then use super glue.

The next section is the most difficult. The sides of the Panther turret were 45 mm thick, and the inner 20 mm had a noticeable weld line, Fig. 7. An .040" sheet would make it nearly impossible to detail this lower half. Therefore, I decided to laminate two pieces of plastic. I roughed the upper edge of one piece to replicate weld lines. I then glued the two together and attached them to the turret. Apply solvent glue, position them, then super glue them in place.

I repeated this step on the opposite side. I treated the two rear side plates the same, except the triple-faceted rear face has a rough cut across its width. I detailed this after the plates were installed, again with the motor tool. Reinforce the joint between the

two side walls on the inside so the gentle curve of the outside face can be filed and sanded.

Once the basic turret was completed, I used the motor tool to produce a rough finish on the turret roof. Set the drill to its slowest speed, hold it loosely, and let it "bounce" on the plastic. After the roof has been treated, clean it up with 0000-gauge steel wool.

I sanded Tamiya's cupola flush and then glued it into position. I used an old Nichimo Ausf G gun mantlet with the "chin" sanded off and the inner face reinforced with super glue and baking powder. If you don't have the Nichimo kit, reduce the Tamiya mantlet width to 45 mm; cut 3 mm off each end and rebuild it with Milliput.

I used the Tamiya barrel and filled in the connection with

Milliput. This step is not required if the Tamiya mantlet is used.

For the gun exhaust fume extractor, I made a rough cut in the Tamiya roof, then sanded the base down to the required depth and glued it in place. Fig. 8 shows the completed turret.

Superdetailing. Tool clasps, spare treads, etc., are common to all armored vehicles; I recommend incorporating them in your model. Modelers can choose from a wide range of accessories and detail parts. Verlinden, Peddinghaus, and On the Mark are three of my favorite manufacturers. On the Mark offers excellent variety and value for the money, with accessories for Panther tanks I-IV.

On this Panther there were only two substantial items of superdetailing, the antiaircraft machine gun mount and the traveling gunlock, Figs. 9 and 9a. I used Historex Agents' punch and die set to stamp out links for the chain on the gunlock. These finely machined tools are well worth the price. The engine louvers, Fig. 10, are covered with Verlinden Mesh Wire (No. 48). Cut exactly the size required; liberally coat the area with solvent glue; position the wire; protect your finger with a piece of paper; and press the wire into position. To avoid a mess, don't forget the paper—your finger can mar the plastic.

Superdetailing tracks. In the past, poorly detailed tracks often spoiled the model. Japan has provided the answer with Model Kasten's outstanding plastic individual tracks. To the purist they are worth the added expense.

The first step is to test fit the tracks. A dry run is essential. Split the tracks into two equal lengths. Using solvent glue, assemble all the joints except those that go around the drive and rear idler. Quickly install the tracks, remembering to allow for the Panther's unique sag. Once the glue has cured, carefully remove the tracks.

After painting, install the driver and rear idler, then the top track. Next, install all road wheels, and finally, the bottom track. Glue the front and rear joints with a fast-setting plastic glue such as MEK, available at industrial and auto paint stores.

I believe the keys to improving models are good reference material and the commitment to recreate the details you observe in your research. Graduation from superdetailing to scratchbuilding is inevitable, and not to be feared or avoided.

SOURCES

- Sheet styrene: Evergreen Scale Models, 12808 N. E. 125th Way, Kirkland, WA 98034
- Nuts and bolts: Grandt Line Products, Inc., 1040B Shary Court, Concord, CA 94518
- Punch and die set: Historex Agents, 157 Snargate St., Dover, Kent CT17 9BZ England
- Tank tread kit: Modelkasten, distributed by Marco Polo Imports, 532 South Coralridge Place, Industry, CA 91746

- Milliput epoxy putty: Rosemont Hobby Shop, P. O. Box 139, Trexler Mall, Trexlertown, PA 18087

The following are sources of 1/35 scale armor accessories:
- On the Mark Models, P. O. Box 663, Louisville, CO 80027
- Verlinden Products, VLS Mail Order, Lone Star Park, 811 Lone Star Dr., O'Fallon, MO 63366

UPGRADING TAMIYA'S 1/35 SCALE STUG IV

Simple ways to improve a Sturmgeschütz

Fig. 1. Glen built Tamiya's 1/35 scale Sturmgeschütz IV with simplicity and economy in mind. The sum of his easy techniques is a detailed model.

BY GLEN PHILLIPS

I am not an expert modeler. I fall into that great gray area where many of us are, between the out-of-the-box builder and the constant show stopper. Oh, I have an airbrush, a compressor, a motor tool, piles of sheet plastic, and other specialized tools and supplies, but I've never bought a kit solely to use one or two parts, added photoetched brass details, or cast my own parts in RTV molds.

Frankly, superdetailing scares me—not the complexity, but the cost. I maintain that with sheet plastic, a sharp hobby knife, putty, and patience, you can build better models cheaply. For example, I chose Tamiya's 1/35 scale Sturmgeschütz IV (kit No. 35087) to illustrate my point. Although it's a good kit, it still leaves room for improvement.

I cleaned up many of the kit's parts by filing off mold seams, burrs, and flash. These blemishes are most often found on parts with round sections (such as hand grabs or tool handles). Parts with parallel or perpendicular mating surfaces may need filing to square them off. Take a hard look at each part before working on it—extra effort but the results are worth it.

Zimmerit. In World War II, Russian infantrymen destroyed German tanks by attaching magnetic mines to them. The Germans applied Zimmerit, a non-metallic paste, to thwart this ploy.

Squadron Green Putty

I modeled Zimmerit on the upper and lower hull using Squadron Green Putty, Fig. 3, and grooving it with a ¾" X-acto razor saw. Of course, you could use other methods and materials. However, the saw and putty were handy. (Remember: cheap.)

On long, flat sections, I applied a bead of putty to one end of a panel, then dragged the saw blade across it. I jogged the blade every 3 mm or so to vary the pattern. On smaller sections, I spread a thin layer of putty on the whole panel, then grooved it. If the putty started to set, I softened it with Testor's liquid cement. To avoid mashing the patterned putty, I let each part dry before proceeding.

Front to back. I started at the front of the vehicle and worked my way back, adding and correcting small details. I thinned the front fender edges and detailed the inner surfaces of the fenders with sheet plastic and rivets, Fig. 4.

Looking ahead to painting, I used a knife to deepen hinges and other details. A dark wash sinks into these recesses and highlights details, Fig. 4.

Weld seams. I added weld seams to the glacis plate and the driver's overhead plate with a motor tool and Dremel bits 108 and 109. To make a realistic seam, use a low to medium speed and vary the depth and width of the cut; cut slightly right and left of the weld center line as well. A swipe with liquid cement smooths the seam slightly and removes plastic shavings.

You can replicate weld seams without a motor tool. Run a small

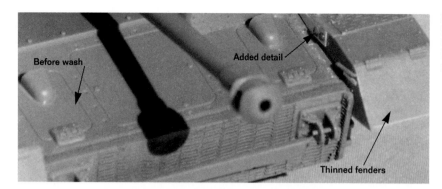

Fig. 4. Rivets are easy details to add. Planning ahead for painting, Glen used an X-acto knife to deepen hinges, panel lines, and other molded details.

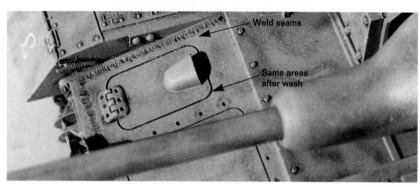

Fig. 5. After the wash, details stand out. Recessed areas are accented because they retain more wash. A motor tool makes quick work of weld seams.

bead of liquid cement along the weld line, wait a few seconds for the plastic to soften, then scribe the seams. (You can use a scribing tool or the back side of a knife blade.) This takes time—a motor tool is my concession to luxury.

Hinges, brackets, tools, and straps. I made hinges for the front fender from three small sections of sprue. I left these pieces off until all painting and weathering were complete.

Moving back over the hull, I enhanced all the hinges on top of the fighting compartment and the rear engine deck. I sharpened the tool retaining straps and made a shallow cut where the tool and strap meet. This makes a small channel for a dark wash to flow into, Fig. 6.

I added all the tools before painting. Then you can weather them at the same rate as the rest of the vehicle. I left off the muffler,

drive sprocket, road and idler wheels, and tracks until after painting and weathering.

Painting. I airbrushed an overcoat of dark brown, then followed it with a coat of standard German dark yellow. The middle of all the main structural panels, crew, and maintenance hatches received an opaque coat of this yellow. The coat became lighter as I moved the airbrush toward the edges of the panels. Then I sprayed a lighter

Fig. 6. A small cut between tool and strap makes a big difference when wash is applied. The brackets holding the wrench are easy to see in this photo.

Fig. 7. Glen replicated rust by adding cleansing powder to the paint on the muffler. Note the exhaust stain above the muffler.

Exhaust stain

Muffler

tint of the same dark yellow in the center of all the horizontal panels. I sprayed a red/brown camouflage over the vehicle, a little paler on the upper horizontal surfaces than on the vertical surfaces. When I finished this session the paint job looked patchy. Subsequent weathering evened it out.

After the paint hardened for 24 hours I applied a dark wash. I do not apply wash over the entire vehicle and wipe it; I prefer washing selectively around bolt and screwheads, in panel lines, on the suspension components, and also around retaining devices. Basically, apply wash to anything engraved into or projecting from the main surface of the vehicle.

Weathering. I dry-brushed with a lighter tint of the dark yellow, then followed with a thin coat (almost a thick wash) of dark brown/gray. The thinned paint flowed around the road wheels, speeding the process. I painted the wheels while they were still attached to the sprue.

I dry-brushed a coating of dust (a mix of earth-tone paints) on the lower hull and wheels before attaching wheels and sprockets. I

usually dry-brush with a stiff-bristled flat brush (about ¼" to ½" wide). For subtle effects (such as dust), use a fluffy makeup brush. This thick brush holds a lot of paint; get all of the wet paint out to avoid streaks.

Rusty muffler. I weathered the muffler with a combination of red and brown paints and Comet powdered cleanser. I used Comet because it was handy. (Remember: cheap.) After giving the muffler a heavy coat of dark reddish brown, I reloaded the brush with paint, dipped it in the cleanser, and applied another coat. When the muffler dried I dry-brushed it with successively lighter tones of reddish brown. Overpainting with the vehicle's base color replicated bubbling paint, Fig. 7.

I used the Super Scale system for decals, toned the colors of the decals down with a wash of black water color, and then dry-brushed dust over the entire hull and the side skirts.

The bottom line. It isn't necessary to spend a lot to produce a nice model. All you need are basic modeling skills and a few easy tricks!

REFERENCES

Chamberlain, Peter, and Hilary L. Doyle, *Encyclopedia of German Tanks of World War Two*, Arco Publishing, New York, 1978

ADDING AN INTERIOR TO TAMIYA'S 1/35 SCALE KV-2

Inside tips for WW II tanks

Dan had interior motives when he selected Tamiya's 1/35 scale KV-2. Plenty of room for details!

BY DAN TISONCIK

The World War II Soviet KV-2, an artillery fire-support variant of the Soviet heavy tank KV-1, mounted a 152 mm field howitzer in a tall, slab-sided turret. It entered action against Finland's Mannerheim Line in winter 1940, hardly an ideal setting for a tank that weighed more than 53 tons. It was a clumsy vehicle. The weight of its gun and turret precluded firing on the move or traversing the gun on an incline. While its thick armor could repel most antitank shells, the greatest threat to the KV-2 was mechanical failure.

When I decided to model a tank interior, I chose Tamiya's 1/35 scale KV-2 (kit No. 3563). The kit provides no interior detail, but wide viewing angles through the rear door and roof hatches make detailing worthwhile. The techniques described here can be used on most WWII armored vehicles. Depending

on the model, interior modeling may be as simple as installing a vision block inside a small, open hatch, or as complex as scratchbuilding an engine.

Driver's compartment. In the KV-2 the driver sat forward and slightly to the right of center, looking through a small hatch (for direct vision) or a block episcope. The radio operator sat behind and to the right of the driver. The machine gunner sat under a circular emergency hatch to the left of the driver.

Start by removing the molded ejection pins and battery supports inside the hull. Next, lay out the hull floor using tread-patterned .030" sheet styrene, Fig. 1. Scribe storage bins in the floor, and detail the panels with wire lift-rings and brass hinges.

Install .020" sheet-styrene bulkheads between the driver's compartment (the front quarter of the hull) and the fighting compartment, Fig. 2. The fighting compartment rear bulkhead is also .020" sheet; detail it with circular engine-access hatches (.020" sheet) and Grandt Line bolts, Fig. 2. I added 1/16" electrical conduit and an engine control panel from my spare parts box.

I pulled the gunner's and driver's seats from my scrap box, too, mounted them with Plastruct angle, and detailed them with folding arms of .010" strip styrene, Fig. 2. I fashioned a foot throttle and brake from styrene rod and stretched-sprue cables and made the steering levers from spare parts.

The cables running from the driver's seat to the compressed air reserve cylinders (used to start the engine in cold weather) are model railroad brass fittings. The air cylinders are from Italeri's Tool Shop, cut to size and mounted on the front bulkhead with strip styrene and Grandt Line bolts.

The driver's instruments and controls (tachometer, speedometer, gear shift, choke, and hand throttle) are stretched sprue and telephone wire. The transmission housing and instrument panels are spare armor and HO scale model railroad parts. I scratch built the radio operator's fold-up seat from .010" sheet styrene and detailed it with Grandt Line bolts, Fig. 3. The radio is from my spare parts box.

I finished the driver's compartment with overhead wiring (Fig. 6), using telephone wire and split 1/16" aluminum tubing for electrical conduits, and made a distribution panel from strip styrene and stretched sprue knobs. I detailed an H&R Products 7.62 mm DT machine gun with a cartridge bag made of HO scale truck springs coated with tissue paper.

Fighting compartment. Machine gun magazines and 152 mm ammunition fill the fighting compartment. A rack with shelves and walls made of .010" sheet styrene, Fig. 7a, holds five circular, cartridge-type machine gun magazines. The rack is 9 mm x 9 mm. I drilled 3/16" holes in each shelf, die-punched 7/32" disks to replicate magazines, and mounted the rack on the inside bulkhead with Plastruct angle and

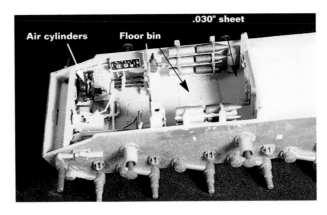

Fig. 1. Scribe bin doors in the floor, then add brass hinges and lift rings.

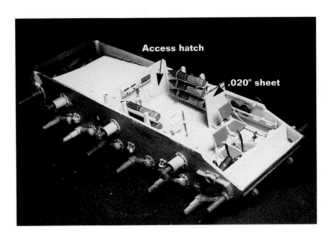

Fig. 2. The bulkheads are made of .020" sheet and detailed with model railroad parts. Keep spare parts handy for radio and control panels.

Fig. 3. Most of what you see is scratchbuilt from scrap plastic and .010" sheet styrene.

Grandt Line bolts, Figs. 4 and 5. The 152 mm ammunition-rack frames are made of Plastruct U channels. I mounted the channels and attached .010" strips perpendicular to the Plastruct as braces for the curved, sheet styrene troughs (.010" sheet). I shaped these troughs in hot water, then divided each of them into two sections to hold the propellant charges and the projectiles. I made two-stage 152 mm ammunition using 7/32" aluminum tubing for the casing and balsa wood for the shells, Fig. 3. Lead foil "leather" straps hold the ammo in its racks.

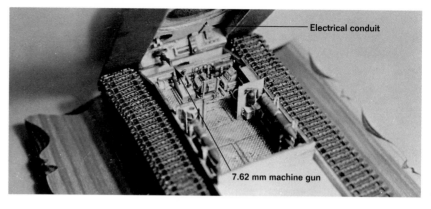

Fig. 4. Aluminum tubing and telephone wire satisfy Dan's 1/35 scale electrical codes.

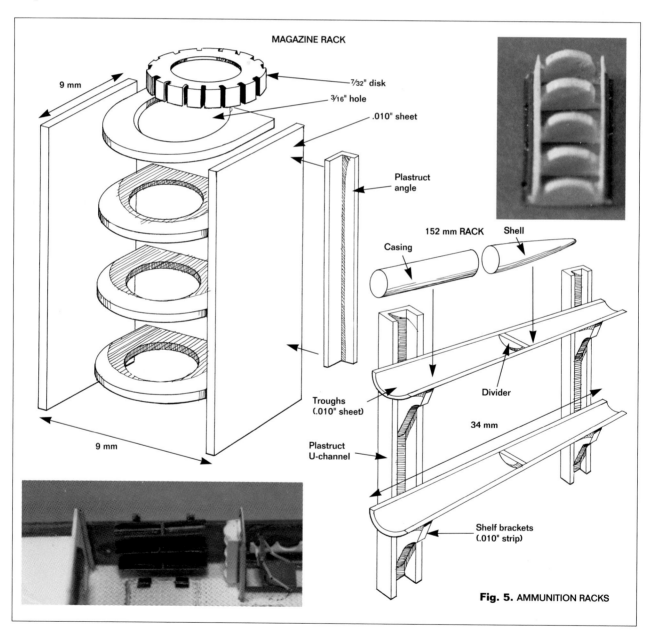

Fig. 5. AMMUNITION RACKS

Turret. Most of the turret was occupied by the 152 mm gun and ammunition. The roof had two PTK periscopes which traversed 360 degrees. There were three side-vision block episcopes, direct-vision slits, and pistol ports in the turret walls. The rear wall mounted a 7.62 mm machine gun with 12 rounds stored on the side walls.

The 152 mm howitzer, with a cartridge-type screw breech block, was mounted on the floor. The gunner used a direct telescopic sight and a simple clinometer (range finder), traversing the main gun by either hand crank or electric motor. As with the hull, start with a floor of .030" sheet-styrene tread plate. (Remember to cut out the kit turret ring).

I modeled the 152 mm howitzer after field artillery of that era, using ½" and 7⁄32" aluminum tubing for the barrel and breech, and four sections of 5⁄32" tubing for the recoil mechanism, Fig. 6. The gun is supported by two vertical braces of .030" sheet "welded" to the turret floor. To replicate the screw portion of the breech, I cut concentric disks of .019" sheet, Fig. 7. The locking and firing mechanisms are made of .010" styrene rods and strips. The clinometer to the left of the breech is from my scrap box.

The turret-traversing mechanism (motor and wheel) is aluminum tubing modified with styrene strips and HO scale railroad parts. I made the gunner and commander seats from .010" sheet and mounted them with .020" styrene and Grandt Line bolts.

I modeled ammunition, racks magazines, and wiring the same as before, Figs. 8 and 9. After carving the distributor box and intercom from block styrene, I detailed

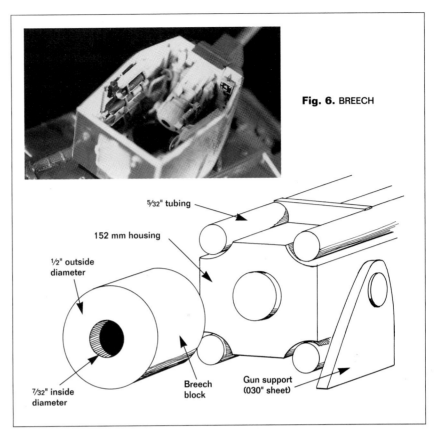

Fig. 6. BREECH

5⁄32" tubing

152 mm housing

½" outside diameter

7⁄32" inside diameter

Breech block

Gun support (030" sheet)

them with dials of stretched sprue. Stowage boxes from my spare parts collection are mounted to the wall with Plastruct angle and Grandt Line bolts.

The turret-ring pad is lead foil textured with tissue paper and white glue, Fig. 10. The open rear door shows off the locking mechanism, made of four strips of styrene and operated by a locking wheel.

Turret roof details include two periscopes from Tamiya's 1/35 scale T34/ 42, turret ventilators (from my spare parts), three episcopes carved from ¼" block styrene, and electrical conduit traversing the turret's top and sides. A sprinkling of miscellaneous field equipment—helmets, packs, hand guns, water bottles—completed the interior.

Exterior. The exterior needed only minor work. I replaced the rear engine screens with No. 60

brass mesh and replaced the rear engine deck latch with scale chain. I replaced the fender supports with .020" strip, added fender braces of .010" strip to the hull sides, and substituted braided lead wire for the tow cable. I installed an M. V. Products parabolic lens in place of the kit headlight and replaced the molded lead wire with telephone wire. I bored out the machine gun barrels and removed the inner wheel braces of the return rollers.

Finishing. I airbrushed the exterior a light coat of Floquil Primer (R9), and the interior a light coat of Testor's camouflage gray (masking the exterior to prevent overspray). A black wash gave the interior a grimy, scuffed look. The interior details are gunmetal, brass, leather, gloss black, and white.

Next the exterior received an overcoat of Pactra artillery olive; I added progressively lighter coats

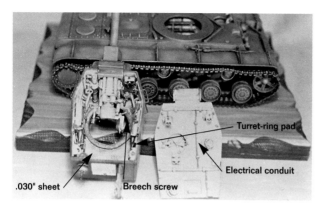

Fig. 9. The 152 mm howitzer is welded to the floor and surrounded by scratchbuilt details and items from Dan's spare-parts box. The lead-foil turret-ring pad is textured with tissue paper.

Fig. 10. Another machine-gun magazine rack and more stowage for the 152 mm ammunition.

Fig. 11, top. The lock is made of four styrene strips and a hatch wheel from the junk box.

Fig. 12. Electrical conduits, air vents, and view scopes occupy the turret roof.

(lightened with white) to develop a subtle, weathered look. I finished by alternating flat black and rust washes. I oversprayed the tracks with Pactra rust, weathered with black and brown washes, and highlighted with a mix of gun-metal and aluminum.

Detailing opportunities. Tank interiors can get crowded fast. Here's a checklist of the major elements that provide opportunities for detailing:

- armament
- communications
- electrical systems
- ammunition bins
- sighting devices
- traversing mechanisms
- crew compartments
- engine compartment

It's not possible to replicate every detail, but with these techniques (and lots of spare parts and imagination) you can more closely simulate a tank interior.

REFERENCES

- Milson, J., *Russian Tanks 1900–1970*, Stackpole Books, Harrisburg, Pennsylvania, 1971
- Scheigert, H., *Stalin Giants KV-1 and KV-2*, Podzen-Pallas

Verlag, Hamburg, Germany, 1979
- Zaloga, Steven, and James Grandsen, *Soviet Heavy Tanks*, Osprey Publishing, London, 1981

SOURCES

- Sheet styrene: Evergreen Scale Models, 12808 N. E. 125th Way, Kirkland, WA 98034
- Scale nuts and bolts: Grandt Line Products, Inc., 1040B Shary Court, Concord, CA 94518
- 1/35 scale 7.62 mm DT machine gun: H&R Products, P. O. Box 67, McHenry, IL 60051
- Brass sheet and tubing: K&S Engineering, 6917 W. 59th St., Chicago, IL 60638
- Brass screen: LMG Enterprises, 1627 S. 26th St., Sheboygan,

WI 53081
- Parabolic light lens: M. V. Products, P. O. Box 6622, Orange, CA 92613-6622
- Patterned sheet styrene: Plastruct, 1020 S. Wallace Pl., City of Industry, CA 91748
- Punch and die: Waldron Model Products, P. O. Box 431, Merlin, OR 97532
- HO scale railroad parts catalog: Wm. K. Walthers Inc., P. O. Box 18676, Milwaukee, WI 53218

REALISTIC GROUNDWORK FOR DIORAMAS

Easy ways to get good earth

Every story needs a setting. Foliage, the color of the soil—and even snow—are important elements in the tales that these dioramas tell.

BY HILBER GRAF

Inferior groundwork on a display base or diorama can spoil an otherwise first-class model or figure. Yet it's easy to model earth. The following methods will produce eye-pleasing results, even on your first attempt.

The right stuff. My favorite terrain material is Sculptamold, a craft product made of cellulose fiber, clay, and a plastic binder. Mixed with water, Sculptamold becomes claylike. It sets in 30 minutes and dries in a few hours.

Sculptamold is better than plaster of Paris, Celluclay, or papier-maché: It's clean, it's easy to model because it stays where you put it, and it dries lightweight and strong without noticeable shrinkage. Additionally, Sculptamold can be drilled or carved, and it takes all kinds of paint well. Sculptamold has a natural-looking texture similar to bare earth. You can mix it with other materials—sand, pebbles, fine sawdust, cat litter—to achieve realistic textures.

Building the base. You can make an attractive, lightweight base with a wood-veneer plaque available at craft stores. A plaque with decorative edges lends a pleasing, "picture frame" look to displays. Use

white or wood glue to attach a small strip of wood around the base's top edge. This ridge contains the groundwork, and it looks clean. Or you can build your own tray of basswood (½" thick for the bottom, ⅛" for the sides).

Whatever method you choose, the retaining ridge has to be higher if your diorama depicts a cross section of a hill or knoll. Saw ⅛" sheet to match the terrain's contour, Fig. 1.

Fill seams with wood putty, sand them smooth, then stain and varnish the base. The varnish protects against moisture from the groundwork.

Creating groundwork. For topographical features, start with plastic foam or florist foam and cover it with a thin layer of Sculptamold, Fig. 2. (Both foams are available at craft and hobby shops.) Use masking tape to protect areas not intended for groundwork.

Put a handful of dry Sculptamold into a plastic food bag. You may add sand, sawdust, or "static grass" to alter the texture. Don't mix up more material than you can use in a 20-minute session. Add water gradually, kneading the bag until the material is thoroughly mixed. Properly mixed Sculptamold resembles stiff clay.

Spread Sculptamold on the base, working it out to the edges with a putty knife or rubber spatula. Unless you're depicting packed earth, don't worry about smoothing the surface. Now install buildings, walls, boulders, or whatever needs to be embedded in the earth. Work Sculptamold up to and around these items.

To model a gritty surface, add the texture materials while the

Fig. 1. Basswood sheets contain the groundwork on a wood plaque. Varnish protects the wood during the work that follows.

Fig. 2. After masking the varnished wood to protect it against moisture, Hilber applies Sculptamold to a foam base.

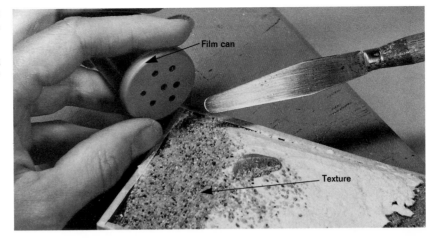

Sculptamold is wet, Fig. 3. Put the texture in a homemade shaker— 35 mm film containers or baby-food jars work great—and sprinkle it generously on the moist ground. Tamp this texture lightly into the surface with your fingers.

After the groundwork dries, gently shake off excess texture. Spray on four or five coats of clear flat, such as Testor's Dullcote, to seal the surface.

Painting. I prefer Polly S paint because it brushes beautifully, dries flat, and is available in realistic colors. Inexpensive ½" or 1" brushes work best for painting groundwork. Unless geography demands a particular color like the red clay of Vietnam or the ash gray of Little Bighorn, start with a dark walnut brown or raw umber. Polly S dark earth (FLP0064) lightened with either grass green (FLP0051) or dark weapon olive (FLP0063) produces a nice mossy brown.

Brush paint on liberally so it runs into all the nooks and crannies. Polly S dries fast, and it's fun to use. Mix a dark shade of the basic color, then flow a thin wash of this over the groundwork. Next stir up a lighter shade and whisk it lightly across the surface, hitting only the raised surfaces: You don't want the paint to flow into the recesses. Follow with progressively lighter shades until the earth takes on a three-dimensional look. The base is now ready for foliage.

Mud and snow. Cel-Vinyl, a vinyl acrylic copolymer used for painting animated cartoons, replicates mud better than anything I've tried. This water-based paint can be mixed with fine sand and static grass to form muddy clumps of torn plants. Allow it to dry until it thickens slightly, and apply it to groundwork or models with a cheap paintbrush or toothpick, Fig. 4. Cel-Vinyl dries to a tough, waterproof sheen that looks wet. It's available in many colors; look for it at art supply stores.

You can replicate snow with baking soda or powdered artificial sweetener. Fix this material with clear spray varnish, sprinkling in layers until the desired depth is reached. Deep snow is fragile, but repairs are easy: Brush on clear varnish and sprinkle more "snow." Combined with Cel-Vinyl mud, the completed effect is stunning!

SOURCES

• Sculptamold: American Art Clay Co., 4717 W. 16th, Indianapolis, IN 46222
• Static grass: Hannes Fischer, available from Wm. K. Walthers, Inc., P. O. Box 18676, Milwaukee, WI 53218

FUNDAMENTALS OF FIGURE CONVERSION

A pocketful of poses

The figures in the diorama above are 55 mm, but with knife and putty in hand (and idea in mind) you can modify any figure.

BY HILBER GRAF

If you model figures, conversions are inevitable. Fortunately, many figures have interchangeable parts. Still, there will be times when you can't find what you need. Converting or resculpting figures allows unlimited creativity.

A battle plan. Consider who your figure is and what it is doing. What emotion is the figure displaying, and how can it be portrayed naturally? Is he running, marching, shouting to someone, grimacing in pain, or rubbing his aching feet? Answer these questions before you pick up your hobby knife.

Pre-construction drawings are valuable aids. Although my own sketches tend to be elaborate, simple stick figure doodles are often good enough.

A basic understanding of anatomy is essential. A head turned unnaturally or an incorrectly proportioned arm or leg can ruin a figure. At college bookstores and art supply stores you

can find inexpensive anatomy guides that are excellent references for figure modelers.

Observe. Watch real people move, play, or simply stand at ease, and you'll quickly learn about natural posing. You can learn a lot from studying yourself in a mirror.

Body language, imbalance, and hyperextension. Body language—a posture, a tilt of the head—can tell a story or transmit emotion. Think of your figures as actors in a silent movie, communicating without words. Slumped shoulders and a downturned face convey one mood; folded arms and a jutting chin tell another tale.

Imbalance and hyperextension are two ways to express action. Suggest motion by posing a figure in an unbalanced position that would only be momentary in real life, Fig. 1, p. 95. Hyperextended figures, posed at the extreme limits of an activity—throwing a grenade or leaping over a fallen tree trunk—intensify a scene.

Frankenstein the modeler. At a workbench littered with miniature body parts and sinister-looking tools, I sometimes feel like a mad scientist. Like Dr. Frankenstein, I require a plentiful collection of spare parts! Using leftovers is quicker than resculpting or scratchbuilding new ones. The same goes for helmets, swords, and other equipment.

Cutting tools rank foremost among my surgical instruments. Razor saws are best for dissecting plastic and lead figures, while a jeweler's saw works well for cutting fragile resin castings. An X-acto knife with a curved blade is especially useful for trimming, cleanup, and small cuts. I recommend the Dremel Moto-Tool.

Often you'll need figures to strike poses that are not commercially available. Using Hilber's techniques, you can convert stock figures to your needs.

Equipped with a three jaw chuck, micro-drills, grinders, and sanders, the Dremel can drill mounting holes, hollow out helmets, or quickly remove details and equipment. It puts a dent in your hobby budget, but once you exploit the Dremel tool you'll wonder how you ever got along without it.

A set of modeler's files, 400- and 600 grit wet-dry sandpaper, and a wire cutter are handy items for your toolbox. Buy a good pair of needle-nose tweezers for handling tiny parts.

Super glue is great for assembling lightweight plastic or resin castings, but five-minute epoxy is

Fig. 1. Posing figures, portraying motion lends drama and interest.

stronger—particularly important for heavy, metal miniatures.

Epoxy putty. Originally intended for caulking and sealing pipe threads, epoxy putty is indispensable for modeling figures. My favorite brand is Duro. It's easiest for me to shape. Duro ribbon epoxy putty is a blue and yellow strip sold at most hardware stores.

It's inexpensive and suitable to use on metal, plastic, resin, and even wood.

Cut off a small section of ribbon (one part blue to three parts yellow) and knead the putty until it turns a uniform yellowish green. Blend no more than you can use within 20 minutes: It sets up quickly after that. Duro can be

applied in thick layers and can be painted five to six hours after being applied, but I prefer to let the putty cure overnight.

Dental probes are nice for sculpting putty—but toothpicks work well and cost a lot less. Keep water handy to moisten your hands and tools while you're working with epoxy putty or you'll find it sticks to everything.

Rolling up sleeves. Let's use a shirt sleeve to illustrate how to sculpt putty. Estimate the amount of putty needed, then position it on the figure. Moisten the end of a toothpick, then use it like a rolling pin to thin and shape the putty, Fig. 2. When you have the basic shape of the sleeve, smooth and blend the joint where the putty meets the figure. Now you can sculpt wrinkles, folds, and other details, Fig. 3. With a little practice you'll be ready to tackle more difficult sculpting.

About faces. To convert a face, make a hole below the top lip with either a knife or small drill.

Fig. 2. Use a toothpick to roll epoxy putty into the desired shape. Moisten the tool with water to keep the putty from sticking to it.

Fig. 3. No need for expensive precision instruments to perform this work. Sculpt details in putty with the tip of the toothpick.

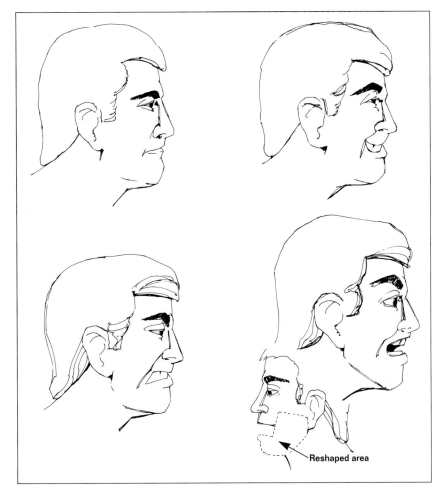

Fig. 4. Face conversion

Reshaped area

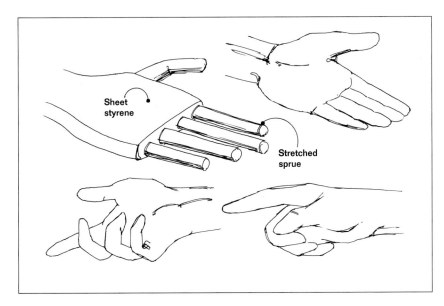

Sheet styrene

Stretched sprue

Fig. 5. Hands

Increase the size of the hole with an X-acto knife to make room for teeth and perhaps a tongue. (Plastic wedges work well for these features.) Use super glue to attach the teeth inside the new mouth. You can build up the chin with epoxy putty. If you're creating a shouting expression, you may have to cut away the entire lower jaw and resculpt it, Fig. 4.

Remember the time limit that the hardening of putty imposes: Keep your working area small. Each face should have a personality that brings it to life. Include laugh lines and other wrinkles.

Hands. Because hand sculpture is delicate work, I wait until other sculpting is done. Cut the hand from sheet plastic, stretch sprue for freestanding fingers, and glue them into place, Fig. 5. After the glue has dried, build up flesh with epoxy putty. On large scale figures (100 mm or bigger), you can fashion fingers from fine-gauge florist wire fitted into holes drilled in sheet plastic.

If the hand is grasping something, the fingers must grip it—firmly. Sometimes I sculpt the hand and fingers around the object being carried, then attach this sub-assembly to the figure's wrists. Varying the poses of the fingers adds interest.

After the putty has cured, fill small surface flaws with more putty and sand them smooth with very fine-grit wet sandpaper. When posing is complete and flaws are corrected, you're ready to install personal equipment and other details.

Details. Epoxy putty is excellent for modeling fine details like buttonholes and buttons. Plan the location of buttonholes before the resculpted uniform hardens and

Replace with florist wire

cures, then cut small slits in the putty with the tip of a hobby knife. Tunic buttons begin as tiny balls of putty which are placed over the buttonhole slits and then gently flattened into disks. Rank chevrons are simply strips of putty cut to length and stuck to a uniform sleeve. Hair and beards are also strips of putty positioned, textured, and blended with a toothpick. Experiment!

Tissue clothing. Thin garments are best shaped from tissue treated with diluted white glue. Thin the glue with water to the consistency of milk. Cut tissue for a section of the garment and attach it to the figure. Use a toothpick to shape folds and wrinkles. Blot away excess liquid with a cheap paintbrush, then brush on a heavy coat of white glue. When this dries, brush on a final thin layer of glue to hide the tissue's texture. To make thicker garments, brush diluted glue over the first layer and add more tissue.

I shape belts from strips of lead foil, and fashion buckles from thin copper wire. Don't forget to check your scrap box again!

Parting tips. Unless the figure is freestanding, drill a mounting hole in a supporting limb, then glue florist wire in the hole, Fig. 6. This mounting wire is most important for figures that are posed in unbalanced positions and for heavy figures. For greater ease of handling, be sure to mount the completed figure on a temporary base for painting.

Always prime your figures before painting. Priming reveals overlooked flaws; with lead figures, it prevents disastrous surface oxidation, as well.

POSING AND DETAILING PLASTIC HORSES

Simple techniques to add life to your equine modeling

The author's 1/35 scale German gun carriage features modified ESCI horses.

BY JIM BERTOLIN

Horses are used in many dioramas and vignettes, yet most of the emphasis is on the figures and the horses are all but forgotten. Horses can be modeled and converted too, so you don't have to settle for a stock horse.

Historex horses. The easiest and most convenient way to model horses in 54 mm scale is to use the Historex system, which consists of almost thirty different horse halves and a dozen heads. These can be purchased separately, and by combining different halves and heads a horse can be built standing, walking, trotting, galloping, rearing,

stopping, or even falling. Obtain a copy of the Historex spare parts list and the latest Historex catalog to see what is available.

I'll use Historex horse halves numbers 1 and 12 with the number 4 head to illustrate the basic techniques of construction. These parts will produce a nice cantering horse.

There is a seam running down the legs (Fig. 1); sand this down before gluing the parts together. Use tube glue to assemble the body; let it set up slightly, then push the halves together, letting the glue squeeze out around the edges. After it dries, scrape off excess glue with a hobby knife (Fig. 2), then file the seams. The head

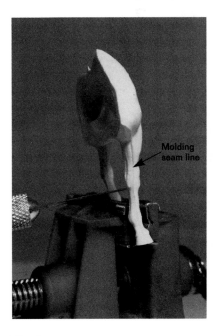

Molding seam line

Fig. 1

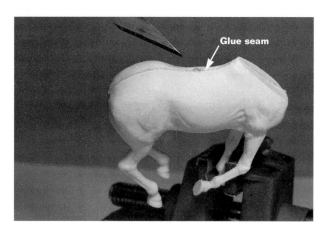

Fig. 2

Fig. 3

and ears can be applied the same way. For the mane and tail I use Weld-On quick-setting glue. This makes a clean-looking horse built stock from Historex parts (Fig. 3).

Converting and detailing. As your skills increase you may want to add details that give your model a little something extra. If you buy Historex figure kits, you'll acquire quite a few horses that are just standing. For a vignette depicting an 11th Hussar at the Charge of the Light Brigade during the Crimean War, I used a standing horse with the number 4 head (plain closed mouth). The horse's hind legs are stopped, but because his head is pulled back, the front legs are off the ground. The horse's belly is then extended,

and his back is contracted (Fig. 4).

To model this, saw the horse in half, taking a triangular piece out of the back (Fig. 5). Glue the front and back halves together to give the horse that compressed look, then reposition it rearing back. I cut around the fetlocks (the joint directly above the hoof) using a jeweler's saw because it allows a nice curved cut (Fig. 6). I repositioned the hooves so they point toward the ground. I cut the mouth off and repositioned it open. This leaves the horse with no teeth, but a tongue can be made of epoxy putty. By fixing only one foot to the ground, turning the front hooves down, and gapping the mouth, I achieved a feeling of violent action. Careful painting,

highlighting flared nostrils and white in the eyes, adds to the effect. **Horses in 1/35 scale.** Historex horses are too large to use in 1/35 scale. While Tamiya and ESCI products in this scale can be used, they are not as easy to work with as Historex. With careful planning and mixing, however, these models can produce pleasing horses.

ESCI offers two horses with its supply and medical wagon kits (Nos. 5010 and 5014) with German harnesses which can be removed with a motor tool. Tamiya has two horses with its field kitchen kit (No. MM-203) that don't have a harness. Tamiya also has a mounted infantry kit (No. MM-153). When assembled stock, it has an undersized neck, an

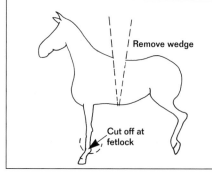

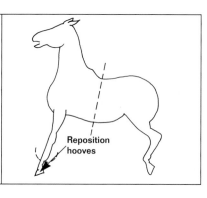

Fig. 4

Fig. 5

Fig. 6

Fig. 7

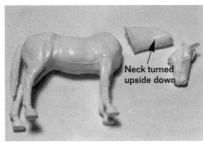

Neck turned upside down

Fig. 8

Repositioned neck and head

Fig. 9

oversized head, and a skinny tail. But the body is proportioned well and the head is nicely molded.

To make a good 1/35 scale horse, use a Tamiya body and substitute an ESCI head. You won't need to file off the harness, and a fine mount with a German saddle will result. To model the 25th U. S. Cavalry Philippine Scout, I cut the neck and head off a Tamiya horse and repositioned them lower. I wanted to highlight the soldier's McClellan equipment, so I dismounted the rider. Carefully positioning the cavalryman draws the eye away from the horse's neck and more to the figure (Fig. 7).

Another way to improve the Tamiya horse is to cut off the neck, turn it upside down, and reattach the head (Fig. 8). This lowers the neck and head and gives the neck a slight arch (Fig. 9).

Caisson & draft horses. Heavier horses were used for pulling

supply wagons and caissons. ESCI horses are an excellent example of German horses and the Tamiya field kitchen set has a good draft horse with no harness. You can apply any type of harness as with Historex horses.

Historex horses can also be modified to represent a heavier animal. Lay one half on a piece of thick plastic sheet, trace the outline, and cut out the shape (Fig. 10). Glue this slice between the two halves, then file around the seams and fill as necessary. The front chest muscles can be slightly reworked with putty and the joint at the neck and body will have to be filled and sanded.

Draft horses usually have short tails and an abundance of hair around the hooves. I mixed a thick batch of dissolved sprue (pieces of sprue dissolved in liquid plastic cement to produce a syrup) and applied it to the legs. After

this was thoroughly dry, I reworked it with a Hot Tool (a woodburning tool with interchangeable tips) equipped with a needle point, using downward strokes. The tail is a short piece of sprue, melted onto the rump and textured (Figs. 11 and 12).

Gun carriage. For my German 7.5 cavalry gun I used ESCI horses, Airfix soldiers' bodies, Tamiya field kitchen, caisson, legs, and saddles, and metal 7.5 howitzer. Though most German horse artillery used a heavier caisson with six or eight horses, I found two photographs of this lighter caisson pulled by four to six horses. Using two different horses, I varied the head, tail, and leg positions. Along with switching heads, six different horses could be built with minor changes. The two wheel horses in a four-horse team have straps across their rumps for backing up. The next

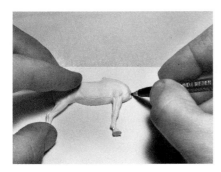

Fig. 10

Sprue

Fig. 11

Tail detailed

Hair added

Fig. 12

Fig. 13

Fig. 14

Fig. 15

two horses don't, so I removed them with a motor tool with a sanding drum attachment (Fig. 13).

I used Tamiya saddles for horses with riders, cutting a square out of the back, adding the saddle, and filling the gaps. Riderless horses have extra equipment added to their saddles. The driver would attach personal gear to the near side horse, so I built this up with epoxy putty (Fig. 14).

Photographs clearly show ropes from the harness to the single trees; I used fine thread for

Fig. 16

Fig. 17

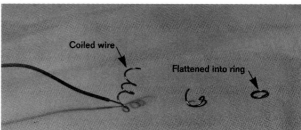

Fig. 18

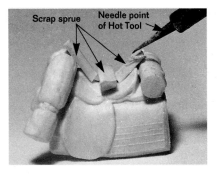

Scrap sprue   Needle point of Hot Tool

Fig. 20

Sprue textured with Hot Tool

Fig. 21

Straps added

Fig. 22

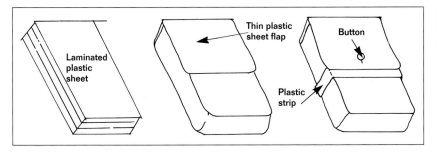

Laminated plastic sheet

Thin plastic sheet flap

Button

Plastic strip

Fig. 19

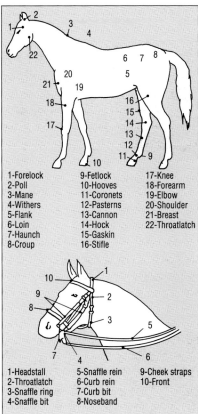

1-Forelock
2-Poll
3-Mane
4-Withers
5-Flank
6-Loin
7-Haunch
8-Croup
9-Fetlock
10-Hooves
11-Coronets
12-Pasterns
13-Cannon
14-Hock
15-Gaskin
16-Stifle
17-Knee
18-Forearm
19-Elbow
20-Shoulder
21-Breast
22-Throatlatch

1-Headstall
2-Throatlatch
3-Snaffle ring
4-Snaffle bit
5-Snaffle rein
6-Curb rein
7-Curb bit
8-Noseband
9-Cheek straps
10-Front

this. Typing paper reins complete the model (Fig. 15).

Saddles, bridles, and bits. Historex offers saddles, bits, stirrups, buckles, and other equipment. You can usually find the type of saddle, or one that can be modified for any particular model, in the Historex spare parts catalog. For girths, breast straps, stirrup leather, and halters, I use thin plastic sheet. Use a straightedge and X-acto knife to cut strips that can be fastened with fast-setting liquid glue. Plastic reins can be frustrating to work with, so I use typing paper applied with white glue.

Index cards work well for the straps on larger scale horses. The headstall was assembled in the same order as a real bridle, with the rings, buckles, and bit made from small wire (Fig. 16), and the bit soldered together. To make rings, wrap wire around the end of a file (Fig. 17). When this is

removed the wire is coiled like a spring. Clip in a straight line to form small rings (Fig. 18).

To make wallets and saddle bags in 1/32 scale, laminate heavy plastic sheet, sand the edges, and apply the top flap with thin sheet. Add another strip over this and slice a button from stretched sprue. A Historex buckle completes the wallet (Fig. 19).

A prominent feature of British and Continental armies was a sheepskin covering the leather saddle. Historex makes a large selection of these. I prefer to make my own using sprue detailed with the Hot Tool. If you want to show equipment hanging out, use a plain Historex British saddle as the base. Apply all the equipment that will be visible (Fig. 20) and attach sprue over the top (Fig. 21). Finally, melt the sprue over the saddle and engrave hair texture (Fig. 22).

SOURCES

• Historex parts: Historex Agents, 157 Snargate St., Dover, Kent CT17 9BZ, England
• Santos Models, P. O. Box 4062, Harrisburg, PA 17111

INDEX